The Eildon Tree - Romany Language and Lore

Michael Hoadley

The Eilðon Tree - Romany Language and Lore

©2000 Michael Hoadley

ISBN 186163 0972

Cover design by Paul Mason
Illustrations by Michael Hoadley

Published by:

Capall Bann Publishing
Freshfields
Chieveley
Berks
RG20 8TF

Dedication

To The Memory Of My Father,
Vague As It Is,
And To The Eventual Realisation
That We Did Love Each Other.

By the same author, also published by Capall Bann

A Romany Tapestry

Song of the Earth - Native American Lore and Legend

Contents

Preface

When I finished writing my book, *A Romany Tapestry*, I began to realise just how much the Gipsy in my soul mattered to me and had influenced my life and outlook. It wasn't an easy book to pull together as much of it was of a very personal nature and I have always been somewhat reticent about my inner life.

Over many years, I had gathered a great quantity of material about the Romanies and Romany life. Now I wanted to make it accessible to others who have an interest in and affection for a unique people. This present work, in a sense, takes up where *A Romany Tapestry* left off. It is a companion volume that sets down other aspects of Romany life.

Rowena Farre wrote, "the Gipsy lives out for all of us, whatever our nationality or occupation, that which we truly are, travellers of vast and windswept regions whose myriad journeyings will only cease with the ending of time".

The Eildon Tree is just one more step on that journey for me.

2

1-

The Romanies

Once, when I was sad and bruised because I'd been bullied by some lads from the village school (singled out because I was different), I sat with Alesandro by his yog as an even mist crept down from the fells.

Alesandro, a Basque Gipsy, pitched his tan in the field behind our house at the beginning of each summer on his way to the Appleby Horse Fair.

I was deep then and dwelt on the larger issues of life when others thought that I should have been giving myself over to childish things.

"Do you believe in forgiveness, Alesandro", I asked.

"Depends", he said, then realised that mine was not a simple question and did not deserve a simple answer. So he wrapped his mind around some thought and his arm around my shoulder.

"Does the worm forgive the plough? Does the cart track forgive the wheel? I don't know, and what does it matter? I will not remember you and you will not remember me when we are both dust. We merely pass each other, briefly touch each other's lives, as nomads in the forest of life. As any Romany knows, we are born and we die and we have little control over those events. But what comes in between we do have some control over. Birth and death are no concerns of ours. They are God's business. Ours is the business of living

3

between those two events. Forgiveness? What is the point unless the one forgiven feels some remorse for offending in the first place. No, let them square their account with God. Did you ever think how alike the words forgive and forget are? Far better to forget."

I learned most about Romany life and lore from the talks that Alesandro and I had.

It would be quite wrong to think of the Romanies in terms of a strictly recognisable racial type. The idea that British Romanies have blue-black locks is a misconception. Their hair is in the same colour range as the Gorgio. Of course, there is a type but there are just as many fair skinned, fair and red-haired Romanies about. Black is the rarest shade accept among those with Latin blood. John (Petulengro) Smith, whose ancestor was immortalised by George Borrow, was of pure English appearance with pale blue eyes. Nevertheless, just a drop of Romany blood is enough to colour a whole life. It used to be quite rare for Romanies to inter-marry with Gorgios (non-Gipsies) but that has not been the case in recent times.

Quite a large number of Romanies do give up the travelling life to settle down. Others only travel periodically. Travellers are still persecuted and moved on by officialdom should they stop to pitch their tan for even a short while. In Britain, officialdom has done everything it can to make travellers settle but, at least, they haven't been murdered or forced into factories as they have been elsewhere in Europe.

Gipsies rarely use the word freedom probably because they are relatively free beings who communicate fully and freely with others and are spontaneous and unselfconscious. Theirs is the extravagant emancipation from all prejudice which was developed by advanced thinkers among Hindu sages. Christianity has avoided the degree of radicalism inherent in

4

Romany mores. Although many Romanies are Christian (predominantly Roman Catholic) they shun organised religion and still cling to many Pagan beliefs and values. Very few Romany tales have a moral. Apart from the observance of certain tribal taboos (and not much of that these days), Romanies are very liberal and regard personal morality from the Pagan perspective that 'and it do none harm, do what thou wilt'.

Among the nomads of Britain, the Gipsies are the aristocrats. Largely based on linguistic studies, it is now generally accepted that the Romanies originated in India back in the mists of time. The Romany Language has a good many words that are derivations of Hindi.

The Romanies are a traditional people with their own customs, superstitions, laws, herbal cures and unique way of life.

Romany women are strong, proud, independent but feminine. They are not servile. Men and women are looked on as having equal though differing parts to play in life. Neither sex is superior and both have considerable power in their own spheres. Women were always the tribal doctors and still are. Men maintain the law and order. Both men and women take great pains over their personal appearance. Men often have their hair curled with heated tongs. Both sexes have a passion for hot colours and gold jewellery. However, the Romanies are fastidious and, despite the travelling lifestyle, are very hygienic.

The Boswells, the Lees and the Smiths are the largest Romany families in Britain.

Romanies look after their own. No matter what their differences, it is an unwritten law that no Romany betrays another or he is shunned by the tribe. Once, the worst punishment a Romany chieftain could inflict on one of his clan was banishment. This fate was considered worse than death. No other clan would accept the outcast and he was forced into a solitary wandering life until he passed out of this world miserably beneath a tree or hedgerow.

The Gipsies love the natural world but do not romanticise it. The travelling life is a hard one. It used to be a common sight to see vardoes hung with drying bunches of herbs and caged birds. These cages contained finches, budgies, canaries, tits, blackbirds, thrushes or yellowhammers. Linnets were popular because of their pleasant singing and bright plumage.

Romanies love music and an evening sing-song around the yog is the usual end to a gathering. A good story, well-told is also very much a part of Romany tradition - an oral tradition. The more fantastical or absurd the story the better. And if the story should be about one of themselves, still better. Adult and child alike will gather around the yog to hear a good tale.

One such episode is lovingly recalled by Rowena Farre in her book, *A Time From The World*. She tells the story of Chaya and Lynndon to a campfire gathering after after a day's fruit picking.

Chaya was a Gipsy girl who fell in love with the Gorgio, Lynndon. The tribe was against their union so they eloped. The tribe pursued them into the Black Mountains. Chaya gave Lynndon a swan's feather as a token of her love. Birds feathers have magical significance for Gipsies. Lynndon dies from the cold and Chaya goes in search of the Eildon Tree. If she lays a leaf from it on Lynndon's breast he will return to life. Chaya still seeks the tree, as do I to bring back all that I lost with the passing of innocence.

It is said that only when the Romanies unite with Gorgios, the wild with the tame, will Chaya find the Eildon Tree.

6

At a deeper level, I think the Eildon Tree is symbolic of the Romanies - a unique and often misunderstood people. The trees roots are deep as is their heritage. The leaves are the pages of their book. Pages of language and lore, medicine and law, songs and stories. Oral traditions, unless set down in ink, that might be lost forever.

"Now, said Alesandro, drawing me closer with his protective arm, "let's have that story".

2-

Romany Tales

The Dead Man's Gratitude

(A Turkish Gipsy Tale)

Once upon a time there was a king who had three sons. He gave each of his sons a hundred thousand piastres. The youngest son took to the road and whenever he found poor folk, he gave them money. The eldest brother used his money to build ships and make more money from trade. The middle brother used his money to build shops and make more money from selling. Then, all three sons came to their father.

"What have you done with your money, my son", the king asked his eldest.

" I have built ships, my father", the eldest replied.

"And what have you done, my son", the king asked his middle boy.

"I have built shops , my father", he replied.

"And what have you done with your money, my son", the king asked his youngest boy.

"I?" replied the youngest son, "I gave money to every poor man I found. I paid the cost of every poor girl's marriage".

The king said, "my youngest son will care well for the poor and so I will give him another hundred thousand piastres".

The boy departed and spent the money here and there until only twelve piastres were left.

On his journey, he happened on some peasants who had dug up a corpse and were beating it.

"Why do you do this", the lad asked.

"We want twelve piastres off him", they replied.

"I will give you the money if you let him be", said the lad. He gave them the money and the peasants let the dead man be. The lad departed.

The dead man rose up and followed the lad. "Where are you going", asked the dead man.

"I am going for a walk."

"I will come with you, we will go together, we will be partners."

"As you wish", the lad responded.

"Come", said the dead man, "I will bring you to a place I know".

The dead man brought the lad to a village. In that village there lived a girl who took a husband and slept with him. When the light broke through heaven's gate, the girl's husband was dead.

"I will get you the girl", said the dead man, "but you and I will always be partners".

The dead man found the girl and, watching her as she slept, he saw a dragon come out of her mouth for she was possessed by this beast and it had killed her husband.

The dead man brought the lad to the girl and then he said to the lad, "and tonight when you go to bed, I will lie with you too". The dead man took up a sword and went to the young couple.

"It will never do that you should lie with me also, protested the lad, if you want her, you take her."

"Are we not partners", replied the dead man, "it is you that I will lie with, you will sleep with her".

At midnight, while the lad lay beside the girl, the dead man saw her mouth open and the dragon came forth. He drew his sword and struck off the dragon's three heads. He put the heads in his shirt and lay down to sleep.

When the girl arose the next morning and saw her new husband still alive she told her father, "today, your daughter has seen the dawn break with her husband".

"And he shall be my son-in-law", said the girl's father and gave her a great dowry.

The lad took the girl to meet his own father. On the way, the dead man said, "come, let us divide the money", and they fell to dividing it.

"Now that we have divided the money", said the dead man, "let us also divide your wife".

"How divide her?" the lad replied, "if you want her, you take her".

10

"I will not take her", responded the dead man, "we will divide her".

Again, the lad asked, "how divide?"

"I", said the dead man, "I will divide her".

The dead man seized the girl and bound her. "Catch hold of one foot and I'll take the other", he commanded the lad. The dead man raised his sword to strike.

In terror, the girl opened her mouth and screamed and the rest of the dragon fell out of her.

The dead man said to the lad, "I need no wife and have no need of money. These dragon's heads", he continued, taking them from his shirt, "are what killed her first husband. Take the girl, she shall be yours and the money shall be yours. You did me a kindness and now I have done you one".

The dead man returned to his grave and the lad and his maid lived long and happily together.

The Three Sisters
(A Slovak Gipsy Tale)

There was once a king who had three beautiful daughters. The three sisters disappeared every night but their father did not know where they went. He summoned his servant, Jankos, and his sorceress, Halenka.

"Do you know where my daughters go each night", the king asked Jankos, "they are not to be found in their room and they keep wearing out new shoes".

Jankos concealed herself by the door to the princesses' room and kept watch to see where they went to. But Halenka already knew and she told Jankos everything.

Halenka warned Jankos, "when they come, they will prick you with needles and fling fire on you. Be still like a corpse and do not stir."

That night, the devils came for the girls and set out with them to hell. Jankos followed at a safe distance. On and on they walked but Jankos did not lose sight of them. She followed the girls to hell through the diamond forest. But she cut herself on a diamond twig which broke and made a great noise. Jankos picked it up.

"Jankos is following us", the girls cried. But the devils answered, "and what does it matter if she does".

Then, they travelled through a forest of glass and, once more, Jankos broke off a twig. She picked it up and now she had two tokens.

Next, they travelled through a golden forest and, again, Jankos broke off a branch. So, now she carried three tokens; one of diamonds, one of glass and one of gold.

Halenka, who had followed behind Jankos, came to her and said, "I will change you into a fly. When you come into hell, creep under the devil's bed and hide yourself. Wait and see what happens". And so Halenka changed Jankos into a fly.

The princesses danced with the devils on the blades of knives and cut their shoes to ribbons. Then, they flung their shoes under the bed and Jankos took them so that she could show them to the king.

When the devils finished dancing with the girls, each one threw his girl upon the bed and lay down with her. Two of the girls gave themselves to the devils but the third girl would not yield.

Then, Jankos, having seen all and heard all, flew away home and lay down by the princesses' door so "that the girls may know I am lying here".

When the princesses returned after midnight they went to their beds as if nothing had happened. But Jankos knew and she went to the king and showed him the tokens and the shoes.

"I know where your daughters go", Jankos told the king, "they go to hell! They dance with the devils and two gave themselves to the devils but the third would not yield. Here is the proof. Here are three tokens from the pathway to hell; one from the forest of diamonds, one from the forest of glass and one from the forest of gold." Jankos laid the tokens before the king then she went on, "and here is further proof". She produced three pairs of shoes that were cut to ribbons.

The king summoned his daughters and confronted them with the evidence. They could not deny the truth of what Jankos said. The king had them executed. Devils sprang forth from the bellies of two of the dead girls and were scattered about.

The king had his daughters carried to the church and placed in coffins in front of the altar. He placed a soldier to guard over the coffins every night. But every night the two daughters that had given themselves to the devils rose up and rended the soldier to pieces. More than one hundred soldiers died thus.

Then, it fell to a new soldier, a raw recruit, to stand guard and he did so weeping with fright.

Jankos came with Halenka to the soldier. The sorceress said, "when the hour strikes twelve and they come forth from their coffins, jump into one of coffins and lie down. Do not leave the coffin or they will rend you. Do not leave it even if they beg you, and they will beg hard, or even if they fling fire at you."

So, it happened as the old woman said and the soldier kept tight in one coffin until morning and Jankos kept tight in the other. And when the morning came, all of the princesses were alive again and kneeling before the altar. They were lovelier than ever.

Jankos and the soldier took the princesses back to their father and he was glad of their return. Jankos and the soldier married, and if they are not dead then they are still alive, and the rest can go to hell.

The Vampire

(A Romanian Gipsy Tale)

All the maidens of a village would gather to spin, to sew and to quilt under one roof and at their head sat an old, wise woman. Each of the girls was spoken for except one. She was very pretty, prettier than those around her, and yet she had no sweetheart to hold her and kiss her. None of the village sparks would trouble with her.

Then, a handsome young spark came to the village and made a play for the lass. He took her in his arms and kissed her. He stayed the night with her and only departed when the cock crowed at dawn.

The old woman saw him depart and she saw that he had a cock's feet. She could not take her eyes off the lads feet. When he was gone, the old woman turned to the girl and asked her of she saw anything strange about her sweetheart.

"I didn't notice anything, mother."

"Nita, he had cock's feet", the old woman announced.

"I noticed nothing of the kind, mother", Nita replied," let it be!"

Nita went home to sleep and when she arose she joined the other village girls at another spinning bee, what they call a Claca in Wallachia. Then the maidens went off with their sweethearts and the young sparks kissed them, stayed with them awhile, and went home.

Nita's handsome young man came, took her in his arms and kissed her. He stayed with her until midnight and when the cock began to crow, he departed.

"Nita", said the old woman, "did you not notice? Your young spark has a horse's hooves".

"Well if he had, I didn't see them", Nita replied.

Nita went home, slept and arose in the morning to do the work that she had to do. When night came, she took her spindle and went to the old woman's hut. Presently, she was joined by the other village girls and, soon, their sweethearts came for them again.

The old woman told Nita how she could find out where her young man went to when he left her.

The handsome spark came and took Nita in his arms again and stayed with her until cock-crow at heaven's gate. Before he departed, Nita stuck a needle and thread in his back. When he was gone, Nita took up the end of the thread and followed it out into the morning. As Nita came to the end of the thread, she saw her young man lying in a grave. In fear and trembling, Nita ran home.

That night, the young man left his grave and went to the old woman's hut. When he saw that the girl was not there, he asked, "Where is Nita?"

"She has not come", the old woman replied.

So, the vampire went to Nitas house and called out, "Nita, are you at home?"

"I am", Nita answered.

"Tell me what you saw when you came to the churchyard. Tell me what you saw or I will kill your father!"

"I didn't see anything."

So, the vampire cast his evil eye on Nita's father, killed him, and returned to his grave.

The vampire came back the next night and demanded, "Nita, tell me what you saw!"

Again, Nita replied, "I didn't see anything".

"Tell me what you saw or I will kill your mother."

"I didn't see anything."

So, the vampire cast his evil eye on Nita's mother, killed her, and returned to his grave.

When Nita arose in the morning she spoke to the twelve servants of the household. "I have a great deal of money, many oxen and many sheep. I bequeath it all to you because I will die tonight. You must bury me in the forest at the foot of an apple tree. Ill will befall you if you do not as I wish."

That night, the vampire left his grave and came to Nita's home.

"Nita", he called out, "are you at home?"

"I am."

"Tell me what you saw three days ago, Nita, or I will kill you just as I killed your father and your mother!"

"I have nothing to tell", Nita replied.

So, the vampire cast his evil eye on Nita, killed her, and returned to his grave.

When the servants arose in the morning, they found Nita dead. They laid her out decently and carried her, as she had asked, to the apple tree in the forest where they buried her.

With the passing of half a year, a prince went coursing hares with his hounds in the forest. His hounds found the maidens grave. A flower grew out of it that was the most beautiful in the whole kingdom. The hounds began to bark and scratch at Nita's grave. When the prince tried to summon them with his horn, they would not come.

The prince commanded his four huntsmen to go after the hounds. They came to the grave and saw the flower burning like a candle on it. They returned to the prince and told him of the flower, the like of which they had never seen before.

The prince plucked the flower and took it home to show his parents. He put it in a vase beside his bed.

When night came, the flower leapt from the vase and became a full-grown maiden. The maiden held the prince and kissed him and bit him. She slept with him in her arms and put her hand under his head. With the dawn, the maiden transformed back into the flower.

When the prince arose, he complained to his parents that he was ill. "My shoulders hurt me and my head aches."

The prince's mother sent for a wise woman to tend him. He asked for food and drink and when he was recovered, he went about his business. When he returned home that night, he dined well and retired to his bed. As he lay between sleep and waking, the flower leapt from the vase and, once again, became the maiden.

The maiden took the prince in her arms and slept with him. She cradled him in her arms and before the light through heavens gate, she became a flower once more.

When the prince awoke, he complained that his bones hurt. The king said to the queen, "It all began when he brought that flower home. Something is very wrong because the boy is quite ill. We will post ourselves on either side of his bed and watch tonight to see who comes to our son."

That night, the prince retired to sleep as usual. The flower leapt from the vase and, again, became the fair maiden, Indeed, for beauty, she burned as brightly as the flame of a candle. The boy's parents saw her and his father laid hands on her.

The prince started from sleep and saw the fair maiden. He took her in his arms and kissed her. She stood before the prince and his parents, a maiden fair, and remained so.

The prince and maiden married and at their wedding feast all the guests marvelled at the maiden's beauty. She bore the prince a golden boy who carried two apples in his hand and the prince was well pleased.

When the vampire, who had made love to her and killed her, heard of her resurrection, he rose out of his grave and came to her. "Tell me, Nita", he demanded, "what did you see me doing?"

"I saw nothing."

"Tell me what you saw, Nita, or I will kill your child, just as I killed your mother and father. Tell me!"

"I have nothing to tell."

So, the vampire turned his evil eye on the boy and killed him.

On the next night, the vampire came again. "Tell me, Nita, what you saw", he demanded.

"I did not see anything", Nita replied.

"Tell me or I will kill the prince you have married", hissed the vampire.

Nita rose up in a fury. "You will not kill my lord", she cried, "God send you to burst!"

In rage, the vampire burst and died. The floor swam with his blood two hands deep.

Nita told the king to take out the vampire's heart with all haste and she went to her child's grave with it. She placed the heart on the boy's body and brought him back to life.

Nita anointed the graves of her mother and father with the vampire's blood and they rose up. Falling into their arms, Nita told them all that she had suffered at the hands of the vampire.

Bobby Rag

(An English Gipsy Tale)

Many, many years ago, there was a nice young Gipsy girl playing around an old oak tree. The local squire, happening upon her, was struck by her beauty and fell in love with her. He asked her to come away to the hall and marry him.

"No sir", the maiden replied, "you would not have a poor Gipsy girl like me".

But the young squire was determined and abducted the Gipsy girl.

When he got the girl home, his mother warned him that he would be marrying beneath himself. She told her son to take the girl to the Hundred Mile Wood, kill her, strip her naked and bring back her clothes and heart to prove that the deed was done.

So, the squire took up the girl and rode off to the wood with her.

It was a wild wood as used to be common in England. A wood with all manner of wild creatures in it.

The squire dismounted in a glade and dragged the Gipsy girl off the back of his horse. Then he said to her, "now I'll have to kill you and take your heart and clothes back to show my mother.

The girl's pleading was pitiful. "There's a wild pig in the wood and it has the same heart as a Christian. Take that home to your mother and I will give you my clothes as well."

The squire was moved by the girl so he stripped her of her clothes and killed the wild pig. He took the pig's heart and the Gipsy's clothes home to his mother and said that he had killed the girl.

When the Gipsy girl heard the squire ride off, she crept along on her hands and knees to hide her nakedness in the foliage. She had hard work to find her way through the wood but, eventually, she reached a hedge by the roadside.

In the morning, a young gentleman came by on horseback. The horse came to a standstill by the hedge and would not pass by it.

The Gipsy girl, frightened that the squire had come back and ashamed for her nakedness, hid under the hedge.

The gentleman called out, "If you are a ghost, go away; but if you are a living person, speak to me."

"I am as full of life as you are", replied the girl, "but short on apparel."

When the young man saw her, he pulled off his elegant topcoat and put it on her. "Jump up behind me", he said, and the girl mounted his horse and rode off with him to his own great house. They did not speak a word on the journey but the young gentleman knew that the girl had been taken to the wood to be killed. He galloped as hard as he could to get away.

When the gentleman brought the Gipsy girl into his house, all there were struck dumb to see her naked and by her beautiful raven hair which hung down her back in long ringlets. When they recovered speech, they asked her how she came to be there and she told them her story. They dressed her in fine clothes and there wasn't a lady in the land to match her for beauty. The gentleman's parents were delighted with her.

They announced a banquet of welcome for the girl to which all were invited.

The young gentleman's mother and father spared no expense for the party. There were tales to be told and songs to be sung, just as we always used to entertain ourselves. Everyone that didn't sing a song had to tell a tale. No one could leave before they had made their contribution to the festivities.

Then, came the turn of the Gipsy girl and the young man who found her said, now, my pretty Gipsy girl, tell us a tale.

The squire, who took her to wife and tried to kill her, had come to the gathering with his old mother. He did not want her to tell a tale and called out, "Sing a song, my pretty Gipsy girl".

The Gipsy girl replied, "I won't sing a song but I will tell a tale". She started,

"Bobby Rag! Bobby Rag!
Round the oak tree . . ."

"No, no", objected the squire, "that tale won't do", because he and his mother knew what would follow.

Go on, my pretty lass, the other gentleman said, a very nice tale indeed.

So, the Gipsy girl went on -

"Bobby Rag! Bobby Rag!
Round the oak tree,
A Gipsy I was born,
A lady I was bred;
They made me a coffin
Before I was dead."

Then the girl pointed out her husband and cried, "And that's the rogue there!"

So, the Gipsy girl told her story to the whole assembly. She told how her husband was to kill her and take her heart home to his mother. And the gentry set upon the squire and his mother and took them out and hanged them.

The young gentleman married the Gipsy girl and she became a great lady.

;

The Old Smith

(A Welsh Gipsy Tale)

There once was an old smith who lived on a hill with his wife and mother-in-law. He wasn't a very good smith. He could only make ploughshares.

One day a boy came to the smith and wanted his horse shod. But the smith couldn't do it. So, the boy cut off the horse's legs, stopped the bleeding, put the legs on the fire, beat them on the anvil and replaced them on the horse. He gave the smith a guinea and rode away.

Taking the boy's example, the smith tried to shoe his mother-in-law's horse, but he bungled it. The horse bled to death and its legs were burnt to ashes.

The boy came to the smith again. This time, he brought two old women. I want you to make them young again, said the boy. The smith replied that he couldn't. So, the boy put them on the fire, beat them on the anvil, and rejuvenated them.

Following the boy's example, the smith tried to make his wife and mother-in-law young again, but he bungled it. Instead, he burnt them to ashes.

The smith left the forge and set off in the wind and snow. The boy followed him bare of foot. The smith tried to send the boy away but the boy would not go. The barefoot boy told the smith of a sick king in the next town.

"We will cure the king", said the boy, "and I will be your servant".

The butler admitted the smith and the boy and gave them food and drink. The smith forgot all about the sick king but the boy reminded him.

The smith and the boy went to the sick king. The boy asked for a knife, a pot, a spoon and some water. The boy cut off the king's head and stopped the bleeding. Then he boiled the king's head in the pot of water, lifted it out with the golden spoon and replaced it on the king's shoulders. The king was cured and he gave the smith and the boy a sack of gold. They took to the road again.

"All I want", said the boy, "is a pair of shoes".

But the smith was greedy and told the boy, "There is little enough in this sack for myself".

The boy left the smith and the smith went on alone. Hearing of another sick king, the smith went to cure him. But the smith took too much to drink and let the king bleed to death and boiled the head to ribbons.

There was a knock at the door but the smith was too frightened to open it.

"Won't you open the door to little barefoot", said the boy.

The smith opened the door to the boy and, with great difficulty, the boy put the king's head together again and replaced it on the king's shoulders. The king was cured and gave them two sacks of gold. The smith bought the boy some new shoes.

Then, the boy told the smith of a gentleman who had a wizard that no one could beat. The gentleman offered three sacks of gold to anyone who could beat the wizard.

"Let's go there", said the boy.

The smith and the boy entered the wizard's domain and laid down the challenge.

The wizard had a great bellows and he blew and blew with it until he had blown up half the sea. So, the boy blew up a great fish that drank up all the wizard's water.

Then, the wizard blew and blew across the fields until it rained corn. So, the boy blew up a great flock of birds that ate all the corn.

Then, the wizard blew up hundreds of rabbits and the boy blew up greyhounds to catch the rabbits. So, the boy and the smith won the three sacks of gold.

The old smith hardly knew what to do with all of his money. He built a village and three taverns and spent all of his time loafing around.

An old woman came to the smith's door and begged a night's lodging. In return for his kindness, the old woman granted him three wishes.

The smith wishes that whoever takes up his hammer cannot lay it down again, whoever sits in his chair cannot get up again, and whoever gets into his pocket can't get out again.

One day, when the smith's money had run very low, a man came to the smith and asked the smith to sell himself. The smith sold himself for a bag of gold and the tenure on his soul to be collected in five years time.

After five years, the man returned for the smith's soul. The smith gave the man his hammer to hold and it stuck fast to the man's hand. The smith went off to the tavern. The man followed the smith from tavern to tavern and found him in the third.

"Release your hammer from my hold", pleaded the man, "and I will give you five more years of freedom". So, the smith released the hammer.

After five years, the man returned for the smith's soul. The smith asked the man to wait in his chair while he got ready to go. Once seated in the chair, the man could not get up again.

"Release me from this chair", the man pleaded, "and I will grant you five more years of freedom". So, the smith released him from the chair.

After a further five years, the man, now old, returned for the smith's soul. He called himself Beng which means the devil. He found the smith in one of the taverns. The smith told Beng that he had called for drinks but had come out without any money.

"Change yourself into a sovereign in my pocket so that I might pay for the drinks." So, Beng changed himself into a sovereign in the smith's pocket and could not get out.

The old smith returned home and retired to bed. In the night, he heard a great uproar in his trousers pocket and got up. He put the trousers on his anvil and started to hammer them. The devil promised to release the smith from his contract and to never meddle with him again. So, the smith let Beng go.

The old smith died and went to heaven and there we shall see him unless we go to the devil instead.

The Dog and the Maiden

(A Transylvanian Gipsy Tale)

There once was a poor Gipsy who had a very beautiful daughter. She was the apple of his eye and he guarded her closely because he wanted her to marry a chieftain. He always kept her in the tent when the tribe's lads and lasses sat by the evening fire and told stories, played and danced. The only companion the lonely maiden had was a dog and he was constant to her. No one knew where the dog came from or to whom he belonged. He took up with the band and from then on remained the maiden's companion.

One day the maiden's father went to a far city to sell pegs, baskets and spoons. He left his daughter with the other women at their camp on the heath and set out with the other men. The maiden was troubled because no one would speak to her. The other women envied the maiden her beauty and avoided her. Only the dog remained true to her. As she sat sorrowfully in front of her tent, the dog spoke to her.

"Come, let us go out on the heath. There, I will tell you who I really am."

The maiden was terrified because she had never heard a dog speak before. The dog repeated his request and the maiden got up and walked with him out on to the heath.

"Kiss me", said the dog, "and I shall become a man".

So the maiden kissed him and the dog was transformed into a handsome young man right before her eyes. He sat down in the tall grass beside her and told her how an enchantress had turned him into a dog for trying to steal her golden apples. He

31

told her that he could resume human shape only one night in the year and, then, only if a girl kissed him first. They talked the night away and when the light streamed through heaven's gate, the maiden and the dog returned to her tent.

The maiden's father returned from the city. He was merry because he had made a good deal of money. When the old man went again to the city, the maiden stayed behind with the dog.

One night the maiden brought forth a little white puppy and, in horror and shame, she ran to the river and threw herself in. Her people sought to draw her from the water, but they could not find her body. Her father would have drowned himself too, for grief, but a handsome stranger restrained him and said, "I will get you the body". The young man took a bit of bread, kissed it, and threw it into the water. The dead girl emerged from the water and her people drew the corpse to land. They took the body back to the camp to prepare it for burial in three days time. But the strange young man said, "I will bring my sweetheart back to life".

He took up the little white puppy and laid it on the girl's breast. The puppy began to suck, and when it had its fill, the girl awoke. On seeing the handsome young man she started up and flew into his arms, for it was he who had lived with her as a white dog.

The tribe rejoiced and marvelled at the strange tale. No one gave a thought to the little white puppy until they heard a baby cry. When they looked around, they found that the puppy had taken human form and was now a child crying in the grass.

So the marriage and baptism were celebrated together and the maiden and her young man lived in wealth and prosperity until their happy end.

34

The Gipsy and the Priest

(A Slovak Gipsy Tale)

There was a very poor Gipsy who had many children. His wife went begging in the town and came back with a few potatoes and some flour but she had no fat.

"The priest has killed a pig", she thought, "I will go and beg some fat of him".

When she went to the priest, he took his whip and thrashed her soundly for begging. She came home and found her husband at work on his anvil. "Dear God", she cried, "the priest thrashed me". The hammer fell from her husband's hand.

"I will teach this priest a lesson", the Gipsy growled.

The Gipsy went to the church and examined the door so that he could make a key to fit its lock. He came home, set to work at his anvil and soon made a key. He went back to the church to try the key and straight away the door opened.

"Now what shall I need?", thought the Gipsy.

The Gipsy went off to a shop in the village and bought some fine paper, patterned and water shot like the cloth worn by a priest for the celebration of the mass. He brought the paper to a tailor friend and asked him to make a garment like an angel's. He looked just like a priest in the garment.

The Gipsy came home and told his eldest son to come with him and bring a large sack. "Catch me about a hundred crabs", he said.

35

When midnight came, the Gipsy went to the church and lit all the candles. The priest's cook saw the light and declared, "My God! What has happened? All of the church is lighted up!" She woke the priest and told him and he was fearful. He pulled on his cassock and went to the church to see for himself.

The Gipsy was standing at the altar, chanting like a priest performing a service. "Oh God, he who is a sinful man, for him am I come; him who takes so much money with him will I fetch to Paradise, and there it shall be well with him."

When the priest heard this, he hurried home to get all the money he had in the house. When he came back to the church, the Gipsy was chanting for him to make haste as sooner or later the end of all things comes. The Gipsy opened the sack and bade the priest get in. Then, the Gipsy gathered up the money and pocketed it.

"Good", cried the Gipsy, "now you are mine!" He closed the sack on the terrified priest and the crabs began to bite.

The priest cried out, "my God! What will become of me? What nature of being is this? Which angel has God sent to me?"

The Gipsy dragged the sack down the steps. The priest cried that he was being hurt. "Go gently with me", he wailed, "I feel that my bones are already broken and my skin is pinched raw."

The Gipsy dragged the priest down the nave of the church and pitched him through the door into a thorn bush. Then, he dragged the priest back and forth through the thorns and the thorns stuck into the priest. When the Gipsy was sure that the priest was more dead than alive, he opened the sack and left him there.

The Gipsy went home to his wife and family with eight hundred pieces of silver in his pocket. He threw off his disguise and put it on the fire so that no one would know the part that he had played.

In the morning, the sexton found the sack at the church door and opened it. He gazed on the dead priest in horror for a hundred crabs had been busy eating him. The candles still blazed in the church and all who saw crossed themselves for they thought the devil had taken their priest.

The townsfolk buried their priest decently. If he is not rotten, then he is whole - and may the devils still be eating him!

38

The Green Man of No-Man's Land

(A Welsh Gipsy Tale)

There once was a young miller who had luck on his side whenever he gambled. No one could beat him. One day a man came to challenge Jack, for that was the miller's name. They played and Jack won. He demanded a castle as his prize and it was given to him. So, they played again, but this time Jack lost.

Jack's challenger announced, "I am the Green Man of Noman's Land. Unless you find your castle in a year and a day, you will lose your head."

Time went by and Jack, remembering his task, sets out in the cold and snow. He came to a cottage where an old woman gave him food and lodging.

"Do you know the Green Man of Noman's Land", Jack asked the old woman.

"No", she replied, "but if a quarter of the world knows, I can tell you."

In the morning, the old woman climbed to the roof of her hut and blew a horn to summon a quarter of the men in the world. She asked them Jack's question, but none knew the Green Man and she dismissed them.

"Go to my elder sister", the old woman told Jack, "she knows more than I do."

She lent Jack her horse and gave him a ball of thread to place between the horse's ears.

When Jack came to the second sisters house, she greeted him, "It has been long since I saw my sister's horse". She gave Jack food and drink and a place to sleep. When Jack awoke, he asked the second sister if she knew the Green Man of Noman's Land.

"I know not", she replied, "but if half the world knows, I will tell you". So, the old woman went up on her roof and blew a horn to summon half the world. She asked Jack's question, but none could answer and she dismissed them. Then, she summoned half the birds in the world but they did not know the green Man either and she dismissed them.

The old woman took her sister's horse and gave Jack a fresh mount of her own. She gave him a ball of thread to put between the horses ears and sent him off to see her older and much wiser sister. But the third sister did not know the Green Man either.

In the morning, the third old woman told Jack, "If all the world knows, then I can tell you". She also went up on her roof and blew a horn to summon all the world. But all the world did not know the Green Man and she said, "Go!" Then, the old woman summoned all the birds, but they did not know either.

The old woman saw that one bird was missing, the eagle. She blew on her horn again and summoned the eagle who she chastised for not coming to her when first she called.

The eagle replied, "I have just come from the Green Man of Noman's Land".

The old woman lent Jack her horse and told him to ride on until he came to a pool where he would see three white birds. Hide there, she instructed, and steal the feathers of the last one to enter the water.

Jack did as the old woman told him and the bird cried and demanded the return of her feathers.

"Carry me to your father's castle", Jack demanded.

The bird carried Jack to the Green Man's castle and when she was across she transformed back into a beautiful girl, for she was one of the Green Man's daughters.

Jack knocked on the castle door and the Green Man came out. "So, you have found the castle", said the Green Man, "I will set you some tasks. If you fail, you will lose your head".

Jack's first task was to clean the stable. But as fast as he threw one shovel of dirt out, three came back in. So Jack gave up. When the girl came with his dinner, she saw his predicament and did the task for him.

The Green Man accused Jack of receiving help, but Jack denied it. So, the Green Man set Jack another task. This time he was given a forest to fell by midday. Jack cut down three trees and gave up in despair. When the girl brought him food again, she saw his trouble and felled the forest for him. Again, the Green Man accused Jack of receiving help and again Jack denied it.

Jack's third task was to thatch a barn with a single feather taken from each bird. Jack caught a robin, pulled a feather from it, let it go and sat down in despair. When the girl brought Jack his food again, she saw that the task was not done and did it for him. She warned him about the next task that her father would set for him.

In the middle of a lake stood a glass mountain. Jack would have to climb to the top and bring back the egg of a bird that lays one egg only.

The girl met Jack by the lake and told him to wish that her shoe was a boat. Jack made a wish and, behold, the shoe became a boat and they sailed over the lake to the mountain.

"Now, wish my hands a ladder", said the girl. Jack wished and it became so. The girl warned Jack to use each rung and not to miss a one. But Jack forgot and stepped over the last rung to get the egg and broke the girl's finger.

Jack's fifth task was to guess which daughter was which, as in the shape of birds they thrice flew over the castle. Jack knew his girl because her broken finger became a broken wing tip and he picked her out from the others.

The Green Man relented and gave Jack his daughter in marriage and a fine castle to live in. But what were the balls of thread for? Or, don't you remember them?

Death and the Maiden

(A Transylvanian Gipsy Tale)

There once was a lovely maiden who lived alone in a hut at the edge of a village. She was quite alone in the world for she had no father or mother, brother or sister, kinsfolk or husband. They were all dead and gone. She did not even have a sweetheart. She never met anyone and no one came near her.

One evening, a handsome stranger came to her hut, opened the door and spoke to her thus, "I am a wanderer and have travelled far and wide in the world. I am very weary and can go no further. Here I will rest."

The maiden answered the stranger, "Then stay here. I will give you food and drink and a place to sleep."

When the stranger had refreshed himself, he lay down. "Now I can sleep", he said, "it has been a long time since last I slept."

"And how long is that?", asked the maiden.

"My dear girl", replied the stranger, "I sleep but once in every thousand years and then I sleep for a week."

The maiden laughed and said, "surely you jest. I think you are something of a rogue". But the stranger was sound asleep and she had to gaze on the sleeping beauty of his face for a week before he awoke.

When the stranger awoke, the girl gave him food to eat and wine to drink. "You are a very pretty girl", he said, "If you are willing that I should do so, I will stay here a week longer". The maiden gladly agreed for she was already beginning to have feelings of love for the handsome young man.

In the days that followed, the couple became very close and the maiden looked upon the stranger as her sweetheart. One night, as they lay in each other's embrace, the maiden awoke in a state of agitation and roused her young man. I have had such an evil dream, she explained, I dreamt that you had grown cold and white, and we drove about in a beautiful silver carriage drawn by six great white birds. You blew on a mighty horn and summoned the dead and they followed us and called you their king.

"That was an evil dream", the young man replied. He arose and said, "now you must let me go. I must be off, for not one soul has died all this while in all the world."

The maiden started to weep and pleaded, "Please don't go. stay with me."

"No", the stranger replied, "I must go. God keep you my sweetheart."

As he reached out his hand to her, she said sobbing, "Tell me who you are."

"Who knows that dies", answered the stranger, "You ask in vain for I will not tell you."

But the girl would not stop crying and clung to the handsome stranger. "I would suffer anything for you, my beloved, but tell me who you are."

"You love me that much", sighed the stranger, "good, then come with me. I am Death! And the maiden shuddered and died."

The Three Dragons

(A Moravian Gipsy Tale)

There was once a man who had three daughters. He took them one day to bathe in a pond. All of a sudden a twelve-headed dragon snatched up the girls and carried them off to a rocky cave. The dragon held the girls prisoners for twelve years. Their father never saw them or knew what had become of them.

A sly fellow, named Bruntslikos, went to the girl's father and told him that he would do his best to find the girls. In return, the father promised Bruntslikos the hand of the daughter of his choice in marriage.

Bruntslikos took to the road and was gone for seven years. When he returned, he asked the father for a horse. He mounted it and rode off into the forest for a year. He came to a tavern where two fellows asked him where he was going and he told them of his search for the maidens. They offered to go with him and he agreed because, he thought, three will make merrier company.

As they rode through the forest, Bruntslikos' horse happened upon the entrance to the dragons cave and scraped at it with his hoof. Bruntslikos realised that this was where the girls were imprisoned. He left his two comrades on the brink of the great cavity and had them lower him down on a rope to fetch up one of the maidens. "I must fetch her at any cost", said Bruntslikos.

He found one maiden sitting alone. She explained that the dragon had gone to hunt hares. Then she asked, "How is it that you came here, my beloved? You will lose your life here."

45

"I am not afraid", he replied.

"Not even a bird flies in here", the maiden added. Then, she thought, 'I will see what sort of a hero he is'. And she asked him to brandish a great sword that lay nearby. Bruntslikos could not so much as lift it. The maiden gave him wine to drink and he began to feel himself grow stronger. Then, she told him to try the sword again and he swung it through the air and cut and thrust with it. Truly, he had no fear of the dragon now.

"Now that I am stronger", said Bruntslikos, "I will soon get you out of here."

"And if God grants that you do, then I will be your wife." The maiden took a golden ring and cut it in half. One half she gave to Bruntslikos and the other half she kept for herself.

The dragon came home. Bruntslikos had concealed himself in a crevice of the rock.

"I smell human flesh", said the dragon to the maid.

"How can that be", answered the girl, "not even a bird comes here. How could human flesh get here?"

"But I sense that a man is here", insisted the dragon, "He would take you for a wife so I will call him brother-in-law!" And the dragon called out to Bruntslikos three times.

Bruntslikos sprang from his hiding place and challenged the dragon. "What do you want of me. I am not afraid of you!"

"You do not need to tell me that you do not fear me", the dragon responded, "I will put your strength to the test soon enough."

The dragon dined on leaden dumplings and invited Bruntslikos to partake. "I don't care to eat such dumplings but give me wine instead", said the young man.

When he had drunk his fill, the dragon challenged Bruntslikos to wrestle him. The dragon drove the young man into the earth up to his waist, then pulled him out again. In the next bout, Bruntslikos drove the dragon into the earth up to his neck and, grasping his sword, cut off all but one of the dragon's twelve heads.

The maiden cried out, "One smashing blow on his remaining head and he will die at once". So, Bruntslikos swung the sword and brought it crashing down and the dragon melted into a bubbling pool of pitch. Bruntslikos cut the tongues from the dragon's heads and put them in his pocket. Then, he collected up the dragon's treasure and had his comrades haul the maiden and himself up in a basket.

When his comrades saw how beautiful the maiden was, they began to fight about who would be her husband. Bruntslikos said, "There are still two more maidens to choose from."

But the maiden said, "I will never desert Bruntslikos. I have chosen him for my husband and we plighted ourselves with a sacred ring, for he saved my life."

Now, deep within the cavern, there was another dragon. (Don't ask me where he came from. Some other Romany must have thrown him in.) And this dragon had fifteen heads and was three times as strong as the first dragon. So, Bruntslikos went back down into the cave to rescue another maiden.

The second maiden showed Bruntslikos a sword that was twice as heavy as the first. The young man could just move it, but he could not lift it clear of the earth.

The maid gave Bruntslikos wine to drink and he suddenly became stronger.

"Why did you come here", asked the maid, "You will lose your life. The dragon will kill you!"

"I came to fetch you", replied the young man, "I have already saved your sister and now I have come back for you."

"If God grants that you may, then I will be your wife."

"I already have one", he answered, "Your sister. But I will as readily help you out". Bruntslikos concealed himself and waited for the dragon to come.

When the dragon appeared, he said to the maid, "I smell the flesh of a man".

"Not even a bird comes here", the maiden answered, "How can you smell a man?"

So the dragon called out three times for the young man to come forth and Bruntslikos stepped out from his hiding place. "I do not fear you and I will slay you", said the young man.

"If you are so strong as that", replied the dragon, "We will wrestle!"

They wrestled and the dragon drove Bruntslikos into the earth up to his waist. Then, Bruntslikos seized the dragon and drove him into the earth up to his neck. Brunslikos reached for the sword, swung it, and cut off all but one of the dragon's heads.

The maiden cried out, "Just one great blow to the head and he will die at once".

Bruntslikos brought the sword crashing down on the dragon's remaining head and the great beast crumbled into dust. He plucked out the dragon's tongues and pocketed them. He had his comrades draw himself and the maid up to the surface.

With two maidens free there but remained the third. To rescue her, Bruntslikos had to face a third dragon. (No doubt thrown into the story by yet another Romany story teller.) This dragon had twenty heads but Bruntslikos defeated him just as he had the other two.

When all three maidens were safe, Brunslikos' comrades turned on him and threw him down a well so that they could have the credit for slaying the dragons.

Before this, Bruntslikos had made a covenant with his bride to be. If he did not return to her within the space of eight years, she should take another husband.

In the eighth year, the maiden took another man to be her husband and the marriage was being celebrated when Bruntslikos returned. He was dressed as a beggar and the maid did not recognise him. He asked her for wine and when she gave it to him he drank from the goblet, put half a gold ring into it, and gave it back to her.

As the maid drank from the goblet, she noticed the ring. She put her half of the ring into the goblet and the two halves merged into one.

The maid broke off her marriage and wedded Bruntslikos instead.

Now, at the wedding feast sat his erstwhile comrades. They had taken the maiden's sisters for wives and had done well on the treasure that Bruntslikos took from the dragons.

"It was I who slew the dragons", Bruntslikos announced to the guests.

"Prove it", his comrades shouted.

Bruntslikos threw the dragon's tongues into the middle of the table and cried, "If they are not dead, they are alive!"

Suddenly, the tongues came together to form a ferocious dragon that snatched up the two villains and flew off with them to the cavern in the woods. There, the dragon devoured them.

And my advice to you is, if you want to slay a dragon, have enough to drink!

The Dragon
(A Slovak Gipsy Tale)

The great city was hung with black and red cloth everyday for mourning. In a cave nearby, there dwelt a dragon with twenty-four heads and that dragon demanded a maiden from the city each day to eat. It was becoming impossible to find food for the dragon every day and the city was in despair. Soon, there was only one girl left. The girl's father was a very wealthy man and the great king, a king over kings.

One day a wanderer came to the city with his dog and asked "Why there was so great a mourning in the place" and he was told, "We must feed the dragon with twenty-four heads everyday or he will crush our city under his feet."

"I can help you with this", the wanderer replied, "It is now just twelve o'clock and I will go to the dragon's cave with my dog."

The wanderer's dog was very big and had the gift of reading thought. Whatever one thought, the dog immediately knew. The dog would have been a match for the devil.

When the wanderer came to the cave, he called out, "Come out here, dragon, I challenge you. You have eaten bread and maidens, but will eat no more."

The dragon called the wanderer into his cave, and the wanderer said to him, "Give me whatever I ask of you to eat and drink, and swear that you will leave the city in peace and never eat another maiden. If I ever hear of you doing so, I will come back and cut your twenty-four throats."

"Fear not, the dragon replied, I swear it. I see that you are a proper man, for if you were not I would have eaten both you and your dog. Now tell me what you would have of me."

"I want you to bring me only the finest wine to drink and meat such as no man has eaten before. If you do not, I will destroy everything that is yours and shut you up in this cave so that you can never get out."

"I will fetch you meat and cook it for you", the dragon responded.

The dragon brought the wanderer such meat as no man had ever eaten. He brought him the finest wine, too. When the wanderer was refreshed, he made the dragon swear to eat no one but sooner die of hunger. The dragon swore and the wanderer said, "Good, so let us leave it."

The wanderer went back to tell the city that it would now be left in peace. From that hour, the dragon never ate anyone. So, if they are not dead, they are still alive.

And what of the wanderer's dog? Well, he made no difference to the tale one way or the other.

So, what of the king's daughter? Apparently, she was superfluous too.

54

Tropsyn

(A Bukowina Gipsy Tale)
(There is also a Welsh version of this story.)

A poor man had four sons who went to work thrashing wheat for a gentleman. Their wages amounted to so much wheat which they took home to their father. "Here father, eat", they said, "and we will go out to service again". so, they went into service with another gentleman who covenanted to give them each a horse at the year's end.

The youngest son was called Tropsyn and the gentleman made him his groom. A mare that Tropsyn cared for gave birth to a colt. The colt said, "Tropsyn, take me. The year is up now."

The gentleman told the four boys to choose their horses. The three older boys chose good horses but Tropsyn asked for the colt.

"What will you do with it?", asked the gentleman, "It is so little."

Tropsyn took the colt and departed. The colt said, "Let me go to my dam to suck, Tropsyn". So, Tropsyn let him go and he went to his dam and he came back a horse to terrify the world.

"Now mount me", said the horse and Tropsyn climbed on and the horse flew. When Tropsyn caught up with his brothers they asked him, "Where did you get that horse?"

"I killed a gentleman and took his horse."

"Come", said his brothers, "we must hurry to escape."

Night fell as they were passing a meadow. They saw the light of a fire and made for it. An old witch sat beside the fire. Her house stood beyond at the edge of the meadow. The boys passed on to the house, dismounted and entered.

"A good night to you", Tropsyn greeted the old woman's four daughters, "can you give us a night's lodging?"

"Our mother is not at home", said one girl, "you had better ask her when she returns."

When the old witch returned she asked what the young fellows wanted.

"We want the hands of your daughters in marriage", Tropsyn replied.

"Good", said the old woman. She made them a bed on the ground with its head to the threshold. And she made her daughters' bed with its head to the wall. Then, the old woman sharpened a sword to cut off the lads' heads. But Tropsyn guessed what the old woman was up to. He took his brothers' caps and put them on the girls' heads as they lay sleeping.

The old woman arose in the middle of the night and felt around for the boys' caps and each time she found one, she struck off the head beneath it, and killed her daughters.

Tropsyn roused his brothers and urged them to be off. As they were leaving, Tropsyn saw that the witch had a golden bird in a cage. He said to his horse, "I will take a feather from the bird."

"Don't", said the horse.

"I will!" Tropsyn exclaimed. He plucked a feather and put it in his pocket.

The four boys mounted their horses and rode away to a city. The count of that city asked them where they were going.

"We are going to seek service", they replied.

"Take service with me", said the count.

The count was unmarried and had a great house. He gave each of the boys a place in his service. He set one to tend his horses, one to tend his swine, and one to tend his oxen. He made Tropsyn his coachman.

One night Tropsyn put the feather he had taken from the golden bird in a crevice of the stable block wall and it shone out like a bright candle. His brothers were angry that he should have such a prize and went to their master. "Tropsyn has a golden feather so bright that no one needs a candle."

The count summoned Tropsyn, "Come here and bring me the feather."

Tropsyn gave the count the feather. This made the count favour Tropsyn even more and his brothers were jealous. They went to the count and told him - "Tropsyn has said that he can bring you back the golden bird alive."

The count summoned Tropsyn again. "Tropsyn, bring me the golden bird. If you do not, you will lose your head."

Tropsyn went to his horse. "What am I to do? My master has ordered me to bring back the bird."

"Do not be afraid Tropsyn, jump on my back", said the horse.

So, the boy mounted his horse and rode off to the old woman's house. And the horse told him to turn a somersault and he would become a flea. "Creep into the old woman's breast and bite her. When she flings off her smock in distraction you will be able to make off with the bird."

Tropsyn took the bird back to his master and the count made him a lackey.

There was a beautiful lady who came out onto the surface of the Danube every Sunday. Tropsyn's brothers told their master that the boy had boasted that he could bring the lady to the count.

The count summoned Tropsyn and told the lad to fetch the maid or else he would lose his head.

Tropsyn went to his horse. "What am I to do? How will I fetch the lady for my master?"

"Fear not", said the horse, "have your lord give you a small boat and put a bottle of brandy in it. Hide yourself in the bottom of the boat and leave it lashed to the river bank near to the spot where the lady comes forth. She will come and drink and sleep. Then we will make off with her." And it happened as the horse said it would.

Tropsyn brought the maiden back to his master. The count wanted to marry the lady but she would not assent. She became wild and the count secured the doors and put a watch at the windows to prevent her escape.

"Bring me my horses from out of the Danube and I will marry you. Let him who brought me, bring my horses."

"Tropsyn, bring back the horses", ordered the count, "or you will lose your head!"

"What am I to do, horse?", asked the boy, "how will I bring the horses from the river?"

"Come with me", said the horse, "and fear not."

When they came to the river, the horse leapt into the water and caught the lead mare by her mane and led her out. Tropsyn caught her, mounted up and galloped off. The whole herd came out of the river and followed Tropsyn back to the counts palace. The maiden cried, "halt!"

"Let Tropsyn milk my mares", said the lady, "and when you have bathed in the milk, I will marry you."

"Tropsyn, milk the mares", cried the count.

"What shall I do", Tropsyn asked his horse, "how will I milk the mares?"

"Fear not", replied the horse, "I will catch the mares and you will milk them."

When he had finished, Tropsyn had a cauldron full of milk.

"Make a fire and boil the milk", said the lady. And they brought the milk to the boil. "Now, let him who milked the mares bathe in the milk."

So, the count ordered Tropsyn to bathe in the milk.

"What shall I do? If I bathe in the milk, I will die!"

"Fear not", said the horse, "lead me to the cauldron. I will breath out frost through my nostrils."

The milk became lukewarm. Tropsyn leapt into the milk and emerged as a handsome young man. As soon as Tropsyn came forth, the horse breathed fire and boiled the milk.

"Now go and bathe too", said the maid to the count, "and I will marry you."

The count leapt into the cauldron and was boiled to death. Only his bones were left.

"Come hither, Tropsyn", cried the lady, "you are my lord and I am your lady!"

The Lying Story

(A Bukowina Gipsy Tale)

(Romanies are very fond of this sort of nonsense tale.)

Before I was born, my mother took a craving for roast starlings. There was no one to go for her so I went into the forest alone. I found some roast starlings in the hollow of a tree. I tried to reach them out but could not. So, I pushed my arm in further and the hole closed up. I went to my godfather to borrow an axe.

"My servant with the axe is not at home, said my godfather, but I will give you a hatchet. Take care, the hatchet is expecting little hatchets."

"Never fear, godfather."

My godfather gave me the hatchet and I went and cut my arm free from the tree. I flung down the hatchet. While the hatchet was falling, a bird built its nest in the handle and laid her eggs. The eggs hatched out chicks. And when the hatchet hit the ground, it gave birth to twelve little hatchets. My godfather rejoiced and gave me one of the hatchets. I stuck it in my belt at my back and went home.

I was thirsty and went to the well. The well was very deep. I chopped off my brainpan and used it as a vessel to drink from. I put my brainpan down beside the well and went home. I felt something biting on my head. When I put my hand to my head there came forth worms. I returned for my brainpan to find that a wild duck had laid her eggs in it and hatched out ducklings.

I took the hatchet and flung it and killed the duck. But the ducklings flew away.

Behind the well was a fire and the hatchet fell into it. I hunted for the hatchet and found the handle but the blade had been burned up. I took the handle and stuck it in my belt at my back and went home.

When I got home, I found our mare and climbed on her back. The handle of the hatchet cut the mare in half and I rode off on two of her legs. The hind ones stayed behind eating the grass. When I got back, I cut a willow withy and trimmed it and sewed the mare together again.

A willow-tree grew out of the mare and up to heaven. I remembered that God owed me a treefull of eggs and a pailfull of sour milk. So, I climbed up the willow and went to God's threshing floor. Twelve men were threshing oats.

"Where are you going", one asked.

"I am going to God."

"Don't go", answered another, "God isn't at home."

The smiths felled the willow. So, I took an oatstraw and made a rope of it and let myself down. The rope was too short and I had to keep cutting from above and tying on below. Then, I jumped down and came to the other world.

I went home and got a spade to dig myself out with and, when I got home, I gave my mother the starlings and she was safely delivered of me.

"A cock and a bull, you say?" Oh yes, and a real one!

The Girls Sold to the Devils

(A Polish Gipsy Tale)

Once upon a time there was an old countryman and his wife. They had three daughters but were very poor.

One day the old man took his youngest daughter into the forest to gather mushrooms. While they were there, they met a great lord. The old man was frightened and explained, I am not poaching in your wood, my daughter and I have just come to gather mushrooms for our pot.

"Fear not", said the nobleman, "I would willingly give you this forest. will you sell me your daughter?"

"My lord", said the old man, "please do not mock my daughter. None but a great lady would be a fitting match for your lordship."

"That doesn't matter to me, all you have to do is to sell her to me."

The peasant did not name his price so, the nobleman gave him two handfuls of golden ducats. The old man was delighted but, instead of going home to his wife, he went to a tavern and asked for food and drink. The tavern keeper refused unless he could be sure that the old man could pay. The peasant showed him the money and the delighted tavern keeper gave him food and drink. The old man became very drunk and the tavern keeper stole all his money. The old man went home to his wife penniless.

"Where have you left our daughter", his wife demanded.

"I have placed her in service with a great lord."

"And did he give you anything for her?", asked his wife. But he only replied that he was hungry and that the nobleman would probably take their other two daughters as well. So, the peasant's wife bade him take them away.

The peasant met another great lord in the forest and sold him one daughter for a hatful of money. Then, the old man said to his remaining daughter, "Wait here in the forest and I will bring you something to eat and drink. Do not stray from here."

So the old man went to the tavern and was again robbed of his money. The peasant returned to his daughter and gave her bread to eat and water to drink. Presently, a third great lord came through the forest and he purchased the third daughter from the old man. "Do not go to the tavern", said the nobleman, "go home to your wife and give her the money to keep in her charge. If you do not, you will be robbed again."

So, the old man did as his lord said and went home to his wife who was very happy to see the great amount of money he brought back with him.

The first lord came to the peasant and told him, "There is a beautiful castle covered in silver in the forest. Go to the town and buy fine horses and harness, employ some servants to do the work and rest yourself."

The old man did as his lord bade him and took his servants and his wife and set out for the forest. They travelled on a road as smooth as glass in the fine carriage provided for them by the great lord. A passing beggar took the peasant for a nobleman and stopped him. "Where are your daughters?", the beggar asked. But the old man would not answer.

The travellers became very bewildered when they found themselves surrounded by deep ravines and insurmountable obstacles. They had lost their way and did not know in what direction to travel.

The old beggar came their way again and asked them why they tarried there.

"We cannot get out of this", the peasants replied, "we had a beautiful road but have lost it."

"Whip your horses", said the beggar, "and perhaps they will go on."

Off they went and soon they came to the magnificent road again. They tried to thank the beggar but he had vanished.

When they reached the castle, the old peasant was amazed by its splendour. The peasants worked for him and he and his wife took their ease. Ten years went by. Once they had three daughters but they were already forgotten. "I once had three daughters", sighed the peasant, "but I never had a son."

One day the peasant's wife was delivered of a boy and the peasant was overjoyed. The boy grew fast and was very intelligent by the time he was three years old. He was a good scholar and when he was twelve years old, his father sent him to school.

As the boy walked to school, he heard two other boys talking. One said to the other, "There goes the little boy whose father sold his sisters to devils". The boy could hardly contain his anger at school and went home as quickly as possible. He took a brace of pistols and called his father. When his father came into the room, the boy locked the door.

"Father, tell me the truth", demanded the boy, "did I ever have three sisters? If you don't tell me the truth, I will kill you and myself."

"Yes", the peasant answered, "you had three sisters and I sold them. But I do not know to whom I sold them."

The boy sent his father off to town, saying, "Buy me an apple weighing one pound, father."

The old man came back with the apple and gave it to his son. The boy embraced his parents and said, "God be with you, for I am going out into the world and I may never see you again."

The boy came to a field where two boys were fighting. When their father died, he gave one boy a cloak and the other a saddle. When asked why they were fighting, one boy replied, "My elder brother wants to take both the cloak and the saddle and leave me with nothing."

"I will put the matter right", said the boy with the apple, "I will throw this apple far into the field and whichever of you gets it first shall have both the cloak and the saddle."

He threw the apple with all his might and, while the boys were running after it, he grabbed the cloak and saddle and made off with them. He travelled on until he came to another field. Here, he stopped to examine the stolen gems and realised that they were enchanted.

"Carry me to my youngest sister", he commanded the saddle. The saddle lifted him into the air and carried him to the dwelling of his youngest sister. He cried out as he knocked upon the door, "let me in, sister!"

"Twenty years have I been here", she answered, "and have seen no one, now you will break my slumber."

"Sister, if you do not believe that I am your brother, here is a handkerchief that will prove that I am."

On the handkerchief, the maid read the names of her mother, father, sisters and brother. Then she bade the boy enter. "But where will I hide you, for when my husband comes he will devour you."

"Do not fear", said her brother, "I have a cloak that renders me invisible whenever I wear it."

Her dread lord came home and as she served him food she employed a little artifice. "Husband", she said, "I dreamt that I had a brother."

"Very good", replied her husband.

"If he were to come here, would you welcome him and do him no harm?"

"Why should I harm him? I would give him food and drink."

Then the boy's sister called out, "Brother, let my husband see you!"

The boy revealed himself and his brother-in-law was pleased by his appearance. He gave the boy food and drink. Then the lord went to call his brothers. They came with the boy's sisters. The sisters were greatly pleased to see him. With them, came a lovely young maiden who enchanted him.

"Is the young lady married", he asked his youngest sister.

"No", she replied, "she has no husband. You may make her your wife, if you wish."

They fell in love with each other and married.

They dwelt in that kingdom for ten years. Then, one day, the youth said to his youngest sister, "I must return home to our father. For all I know, he may even be dead now."

As the youth prepared to set out on his journey home, his brother-in-law gave him large sums of gold and silver. The youth and his wife departed for his father's house. They had to pass through a small wood on the way. In the wood was a beautiful wand. "Let us take up the wand", said his wife, "it is very beautiful and we can plant it at home." So, the youth plucked up the wand.

When they reached his father's house, the old man greeted them with joy and made his son's wife welcome. After five years, the youth and his wife had a son and as he grew, the wand grew strangely shaped in the castle garden. A party was held for the Christening of the little nobleman and all of the guests ate and drank and made merry.

One day, the young father went to town. When he returned home, his wife had disappeared and so had the strange sapling. It was no tree but a demon dragon that flew of with his wife and son. The young father lamented.

"Why do you mourn, my son?", asked his father.

"Do not anger me, father, I am going out into the world."

It started to rain as the young man came to a great forest and he took shelter under an oak. His wife was concealed within the huge tree. The young man slept but was then awakened by the weeping of a child. "Who is that crying?"

"It is your child", his wife answered. He recognised her and cried, "Wife, listen to what I have to say. Ask your dragon where he hides the key to his house."

When the dragon came home, she flung her arms around his neck and asked, "Husband, where is the key to our house?"

"How could it be of use to you?" he replied, "Alright, listen. In a certain forest there is a great cask and inside the cask is a cow. In the cow is a calf, in the calf a goose, in the goose a duck, in the duck an egg and inside the egg is the key to our house."

"Very good", she thought, "that is one secret I know." Then, she asked the dragon wherein lay his strength.

And the dragon replied, "when I am dressed as a lord, none can kill me nor when I am dressed as a king. It is only at the moment I am putting my boots on that I can be killed."

"Very good", she thought, "I know both his secrets now." Her young husband who stood by covertly wrapped in his cloak of invisibility heard the secrets too.

Now, we Romanies kindle a feather to invoke the supernatural and the young lord did so. All three of his demonic brothers-in-law stood beside him. They laid in wait until the dragon was drawing on his boots and, then, they slew him. Then, they went to the forest and found the cask and smashed it. They killed the cow that was inside of it, they killed the calf, they killed the goose, they killed the duck and broke the egg. They drew out the key and the three devils gave it to their young brother-in-law. He took the key and went back to the great oak tree. He opened the door and let his wife out. They returned to his fathers castle and his father was joyous in his welcome. Now that your mother and I are old, keep you here with us, he said. And they all dwelt together and no evil came near them again.

Made Over to the Devil

(A Bukowina Gipsy Tale)

A rich man was driving through the forest when his carriage became mired in a bog and he fell in. Now, his wife's time had come and she brought forth a son but the rich man knew it not. The Devil came to him and said, "What will you give me if I pull you out?"

"I will give you whatever you want."

"Give me what you have at home."

"I have horses and oxen."

"Give me that which you have not seen."

"I will", said the rich man.

And the rich man made a covenant and the Devil pulled him from the bog. By the time he reached home, he had forgotten the bargain that he struck.

When the rich man's son reached twenty, it was time for the covenant to be honoured.

"Make me a cake, mother, I am off to the place my father pledged me to."

So the youth travelled over the mountains to the Devil's palace. There was an old woman and the Devil's daughter there and the daughter asked the young man, "Why have you come here?"

71

"I have come to serve my lord."

The girl was pleased with him. "He is my father. He will turn himself into a horse and tell you to mount and travel the world. Make yourself an iron club and an iron curry-comb for the Devil is powerless against iron. Hit him with the club for he will not stop. Get on his back and keep hitting him."

So, the youth travelled the world on the Devil's back and came home. He put the horse in the stable and went to the maiden.

"My father did not throw you off?"

"No, for I kept hitting him."

The Devil called the youth. He took up a jar of poppy-seed and tipped out onto the ground. "Gather up all the seed and fill the jar. If you fail, I will cut off your head!"

The youth went to the maiden and wept.

"Why do you weep?"

"Your father has told me to fill the jar with poppy-seed. If I fail, he will cut off my head!"

"Fear not", said the maid. And she went outside and gave a whistle. All the mice came to her. "What do you want of us, mistress?", they asked.

"Gather up the poppy-seed and fill the jar." So, the mice picked up the grains one by one and filled the jar.

When the Devil saw the jar he said, "You are a clever chap. Here is one more task for you. Drain the marsh, plough it, sow the corn, and bring me roasted maize tomorrow. If you fail, I will cut off your head!"

The youth went to the maiden and wept. "Your father has told me to drain the marsh and bring him roasted maize by tomorrow or he will cut off my head."

"Fear not", said the maid. She took up a fiery whip and went outside. She struck the marsh once and it dried up. She struck it a second time and it was ploughed. She struck it a third time and it was sown. Then, she struck it a fourth time and the maize was roasted. In the morning, the youth gave the maize to the Devil.

Then, the maid took the youth aside. "He will make me into three maidens and make us all alike. He will ask you to guess which is the eldest daughter, which the middle, and which the youngest. But you will not be able to guess because we will all be alike. I will keep tapping one foot so that you will know."

The youth performed this task also to the Devil's amazement. "I have another task for you, said the Devil, "fell the whole forest and stack it by tomorrow."

The young man went to the maid and told her of this latest task. "Do you have a mother or a father?"

"I have."

"Then let us flee to them, for my father will kill you. Take the whetstone and take the comb. I will bring a towel."

They fled and the Devil saw that the forest was not felled and called for the young man. But there was neither lad nor maiden and the Devil was furious. He set his guards to pursue them.

The youth and the maid saw them coming and the maid said, "I will turn myself into a field of wheat and you stand by and look into the field."

The guards halted and asked the young man, "Did a maid and a lad pass by here?"

"Yes, they passed when I was sowing the wheat."

"Let us go back", said their leader, "we will not catch them now."

When the guard told the Devil that they could not catch the runaways, the Devil asked them if they had seen anything on the road.

"We saw a field of wheat and a peasant."

"Go back, you fools. The field was my daughter and the young man was the peasant."

When the young couple saw the guards coming for them again, the maiden said, "I will turn myself into an old church and you into a monk. When they ask if you have seen a maid and a lad, you will say that they passed by you just as the church was being built."

The youth did as the maid had instructed him. "Go back", said the guard, "we will never catch them now for the church is old and they passed by when it was begun."

When the Devil heard this he was enraged. "The lad was the monk and the church was my daughter. I will go after them myself!"

They saw the Devil coming and the girl cried out, "Fling the comb!"

The youth flung the comb and it became a great forest that reached from Earth to sky. While the Devil gnawed his way through the forest, they got further away.

The Devil was catching up with them when the girl cried, "Fling the whetstone!" It became a rock that rested between Earth and Heaven. While the Devil was making a hole in the rock, the couple got further away.

The Devil was catching up with them again. The girl flung the towel and it became a great body of water with a mill beside it.

The Devil cried out, "how did you cross the water?"

"I put the millstone around my neck", answered his daughter, "and jumped in". And the Devil did likewise and went straight to the bottom of the lake.

The youth returned to his father with the maiden and his father rejoiced..

But the maiden said, "I go to expiate my father's sins, for I drowned him. I will be gone for three years."

She took off her ring and broke it in half and gave the youth one half saying, "keep it safe and do not lose it". And she departed.

In time, the youth forgot his first love and prepared to marry another. A great celebration was prepared just as the three years expired. The maiden came to the feast but the youth did not recognise her. He gave her to drink from the wedding cup and as she drank she placed her half of the ring in it. She gave it back to him and he saw the ring. He took it up and matched it to his own.

"This is she who saved me from death, he cried, I will marry her!"

The Red King and the Witch

(A Romanian Gipsy Tale)

The Red King bought ten ducats worth of victuals. He had them cooked and put in a press. He locked the press and posted guards to watch over the victuals from night to night.

When the morning came all the food was gone, the platters were bare. "I will give half my kingdom to anyone who can guard the press and keep the food from going missing."

Now, the Red King had three sons. The eldest son thought, "Why should a stranger have half my father's kingdom? It would be better for me to watch. Be it according to God's will." He told his father that he would stand guard.

The Red King agreed, "But don't be frightened by what you might see."

As well as three sons, the Red King also had a little daughter who was a changeling but no one knew this.

The eldest son took his place by the press and lay his head upon a pillow there. A warm breeze lulled him to sleep. While he slept, his little sister arose, turned a somersault, and her nails became like an axe and her teeth like a shovel. She opened the cupboard and ate everything. Then she became a child again and returned to her cradle. When the lad awoke, he told his father that he had seen nothing. His father looked into the press and saw that all the food was gone again. In annoyance, the Red King said to his eldest son, "It would take a better man than you!"

Then, the Red King's middle son said, "I will watch the press tonight."

"Be it unto you according to God's will", answered the Red King.

So, the middle son took his pillow and went to lay by the press which had been revictualed. At the stroke of ten a warm breeze came and lulled the boy to sleep. His sister unwound herself from her swaddling-bands, rose up and turned a somersault, and her teeth became like a shovel and her nails like an axe. She went to the press, opened it, and ate everything she found there. Then, she turned another somersault and went back to her cradle, a baby once more.

Day broke and the middle son arose. When his father saw the empty press again he asked the lad what he had seen. "I saw nothing, father", the lad answered.

"It would take a better man than you are", cried the king, "and even he might not succeed if he were as poor a creature as you are."

The Red King's youngest son came to him. "Hail father, I will watch the press tonight."

"Be not afraid by what you see", answered the king, "be it unto you according to God's will."

So the youngest son took his pillow and four needles and lay down by the press. He stuck the four needles in four places and when sleep began to seize him, he knocked against the needles and they sharply kept him awake until ten o'clock.

His sister arose from her cradle and he saw her. As he watched, she turned a somersault and her teeth became like a shovel and her nails like an axe. She went to the press and ate up everything, leaving the platters bare. Then, she turned another somersault and returned to her cradle.

When the youngest son saw this he was frightened and daybreak seemed ten years away. As the morning came, he arose and went to his father.

"And Peterkin", asked the king, "what did you see?"

"What did I see? What did I see?" Peterkin repeated in fright. "Give me money and a horse fit to carry me and the money, for I am away to marry."

The Red King gave his youngest son a couple of sacks of ducats and put them on a sturdy horse.

Peterkin rode off to the outskirts of the city where he dug a hole. He made a chest of stone, put the money in it and buried it there. He placed a stone cross above it and rode off. He journeyed for eight years and came to the Queen of the Birds.

"Where are you going?", asked the queen.

"I am going where there is neither death nor old age, to marry."

"Here is neither death nor old age", replied the queen.

"And why is neither death nor old age here", asked Peterkin.

Then, the queen said to him, "When I whittle away the wood of all this forest, then old age and death will come to take me."

"And one day", Peterkin replied, "old age and death will come to take me also."

So, Peterkin travelled on and he journeyed for eight years until he came to the Palace of Copper. There, he met a maiden who kissed him and took him saying, "I have waited long for you."

The maid put Peterkin's horse in the stable and he spent the night with her. When he arose in the morning, he saddled his horse. The maiden began to weep and asked him, "Why are you going away?"

"I am going where there is neither death nor old age."

"But here is neither death nor old age", replied the maiden.

"How is this so?", asked Peterkin.

"Only when these forests and mountains are levelled will death come."

"This is no place for me", responded the lad and rode away.

"Then", said his horse, "whip me four times and whip yourself twice for you have come to the Plain of Regret. Regret will seize you and cast you down, horse and all. So ride fast to escape!"

Peterkin rode on until he came to a hut. In the hut was a boy who appeared to be not much more than ten years old.

"What do you seek, Peterkin?", asked the boy.

"I seek a place where there is neither death nor old age."

"Here is neither death nor old age", replied the boy, "I am the Wind."

And Peterkin said, "Never will I go from here". He dwelt there for a hundred years and never grew old during that time. He went out to hunt in the Mountains of Gold and Silver and there was so much game he could scarce carry it home.

And the Wind advised him, "Go to the Mountains of Gold and Silver but do not go to the Mountain of Regret or the Valley of Grief."

But Peterkin ignored the Wind's advice and went to the Mountain of Regret and the Valley of Grief. Grief cast him down and made him weep. He went to the Wind and said, "I will stay no longer. I am going home to my father."

"Go not", said the Wind, "your father is dead and your brothers have left home. A million years have come and gone and where your father's house stood is but a melon patch. I passed by it just an hour ago."

But Peterkin departed and arrived once again at the Palace of Copper. Only one stick of the forest remained and, as he knocked upon her door, the maiden cut it and died as it fell. He buried her and rode away.

Peterkin came to the Queen of the Birds in the great forest. Only one tree remained.

"Peterkin", said the queen. "you are quite young."

"Do you remember you told me to tarry here", he reminded her.

The queen felled the last tree and fell with it and died.

Peterkin came to the place where once stood his father's palace. He marvelled and said, "Oh God, you are mighty!" He saw his father's well and went to it. His sister, the witch, came up from the well and said, "I have waited a long time for you, dog!" As she rushed to devour him, he made the sign of the cross and she perished. (This particular sign is the swastika, which in its reversed form used to mean good luck.)

He departed from that sad ruin and came upon an old man with a long white beard.

"Old father", asked Peterkin, "where is the palace of the Red King? I am his son."

"My father's father told me about the Red King. His city is no more. Can't you see it is gone? How can you be the Red King's son?"

"It is not twenty years since I left. How can it be that you do not know my father?"

"Follow me if you do not believe me", the old man answered.

And the old man went with Peterkin to the place where stood the stone cross. Peterkin dug up the stone chest. On one end sat Old Age, weeping, and on the other end sat Death, smiling.

Then, Old Age said, "lay hold of him, Death!"

"Lay hold of him yourself", cried Death.

And Old Age laid hold of him in front, and Death behind and they pushed and pulled. Peterkin became old and grey and wrinkled and, then, he died. The old man buried him beneath the stone cross and took the money and his horse.

Regret is the reward for a life unlived and grief the price for not loving.

The Deluded Dragon

(A Bukowina Gipsy Tale)

An old man had a great many children, He and his family made their home in a cave in the forest. One day he said to his wife, make me a honey-cake, I will go and earn something.

The old man went out into the forest and found a well. Beside the well was a table. He laid the cake on the table and the crows came and ate it while he slept beside the well, the foolish man. When he arose, he saw the flies eating the crumbs. He struck a blow and killed a hundred flies. On the table he wrote that he had killed a hundred souls with one blow. Then, he lay down to sleep again.

A dragon came with a buffalo's skin to draw water from the well. He saw what was written on the table, he saw the old man and he was afraid. The old man awoke, saw the dragon and was afraid too.

"Let us become brothers", said the dragon in awe of the old man.

And they swore that they would be Brothers of the Trushul (the Romany cross, trident of Siva.)

The dragon drew his water and, then, said, "Come with me to my place, brother."

They walked along a narrow footpath with the old man walking in front. When the dragon exhaled, he drove the old man forward, and when he inhaled, he pulled the old man back. The dragon said, "why do you sometimes leap forward and sometimes come back?"

"I was wondering whether or not to kill you", replied the old man.

"Stay, brother", cried the dragon. "I will go first and you walk behind, perhaps you will change your mind."

Presently, they came to a cherry tree. Here, said the dragon, have some cherries. The old man helped himself from the lower branches and the dragon climbed up to eat from the top. "Come up," said the dragon, "they are better up here."

"No they aren't, the birds have defiled them!"

"Catch hold of this bough."

When the old man did so, the dragon let go of it and jerked the old man up. The old man fell on a hare and caught it.

"Was the bough too strong for you?", asked the dragon.

"No", replied the old man, "I sprang of my own accord. I saw this hare but did not have time to run and catch it so I sprang at it instead."

The dragon came down and the old man went to his palace with him. The old man offered the hare to the dragon's wife and she accepted it.

"Say nothing to him", the dragon whispered to his wife, "or else he will kill us. He has killed a hundred souls with one blow."

Then the dragon said to the old man, "Go and fetch water, brother."

The old man took up a spade and the buffalo's hide and went to the well where he started digging all around it.

"What are you doing, brother?"

"I am digging up the well to carry it home."

"Don't destroy the spring, I will draw the water myself."

The dragon drew the water, took the old man by the hand and led him home. Then, he asked the old man to go to the forest to fetch a tree. The old man stripped bark and made himself a rope with which he bound the trees.

"What are you doing, brother?"

"I am taking up the whole forest to carry it home."

"Don't destroy the forest, I will fetch the tree myself." And the dragon took up a tree and shouldered it home.

"Oh what shall we do wife", said the dragon, "if we anger him, he will kill us."

"Take up a big club", she said, "and hit him on the head with it."

But the old man heard them plotting. He took a beetle, dressed it in his coat and hat, and put it on the bench where he was to sleep. Then, he lay down under the bench.

The dragon took up the club and felt for the old man's hat in the dark and struck. Then, the old man arose, removed the beetle and took its place. He scratched his head. "God will punish you and your household, brother", said the old man, "a flea has bitten me on the head."

"Do you hear that, wife? I hit him with this club and he says that it was a flea that bit him. What shall we do?"

"Give him a sackful of money if he will go away."

"Take this money, brother, and go", said the dragon.

"I carried my present to you myself", replied the old man, "you should carry yours."

The dragon took up the sack on his shoulders and carried it for the old man. When they neared the old man's cave, he said, "wait here while I go to tie up the dogs or they will devour you". The old man went to his children and told them to say, "mother, father is bringing home a dragon for us to eat."

The dragon heard them, flung down the sack and fled. In his fright he met a fox.

"Where do you fly to, dragon?"

"I am flying from the old man who will kill me."

"Fear not," said the fox, "he is so weak, I will kill him."

The children came out and cried, "Mother, the fox is bringing us the dragon skin that he owed us to cover our cave with."

The dragon caught up the fox, took flight and dashed it to Earth. Then, the dragon flew away home.

The old man used the money to build himself a house and to buy cattle and oxen and his family wanted for nothing.

The Deceitful Friend
(An English Gipsy Tale)

There once were two Roms. One was a true friend and the other was a false one. But I've run clear ahead of my story.

Micah was true of heart, brave of soul and of a trusting mind. He went in search of the River of Peace. After many days' journey, he pitched his tan near the encampment of some other inhabitants of Rommanipen. And as he sat by his yog another Rommani chal distilled from the shadows and asked if he could sit there too.

Gipsies love company, each other's, but can be suspicious of strangers. But here was another chal fair of face with a ready-preened charm. And Micah made conversation with Georgio, for that was his name.

"So where are you bound for", asked Georgio.

"I seek the River of Peace", Micah answered, "for when one drinks of its water there comes wisdom and riches as well." But Micah's wisdom was the knowledge of the soul and the wealth he spoke of was the riches of the heart. Georgio saw only gold and silver and the cunning to hockaben, for he had bengis his zi.

"I will go with you", said Georgio, "and be your ba, friend and brother."

Micah felt joy for he had travelled much alone in life without a friend. So, Micah shared his bread and mookerimungeri with Georgio and gave his friend room to sleep in his tan. And Georgio hugged Micah and Micah believed that there was warmth and truth in that embrace.

89

At heaven's gate, they packed up the tan and victuals and set off in quest of the River of Peace. Georgio said he'd wrenched his shoulder fruit picking, so Micah had all the gear to carry. But Georgio's easy chat and company seemed to lighten Micah's load. And as the day wore on, Micah grew more fond of his new-found friend for Micah was without guile and looked for no bad in anyone.

Toward evening, the travellers came to a dense wood. It was so thick and dark that they could not see a way through. So Micah put down his burden and sat with Georgio to rest.

As Micah was wondering what to do next, a crow perched on his shoulder and whispered in his ear, "Follow the light of Gods lantern."

"But how shall I see this light?"

"With the eye of faith."

Presently, Micah saw a light shining through the trees and rose up to follow. Georgio was bewildered. He had no faith and saw nothing. He clung to Micah's coat tail and followed Micah along a clearly defined trail through the wood.

When they were through the wood and in a meadow on the far side, Micah pitched their tan for the night.

By mid-morning, the travellers came to a range of rocky mountains whose peaks were lost in the clouds. They sat down to rest and as Micah wondered how they would pass over the mountains a rabbit squatted beside him and whispered, "Listen for the voice of God".

"And how shall I hear his voice?"

"With the ears of truth."

Micah prayed silently and listened. Presently, he heard a sighing sound that gently sang like the wind through a tunnel. Following the sound, Micah and Georgio came to the mouth of a cave. But Georgio had heard nothing. He never spoke the truth, so he never heard it. So Georgio clung to Micah's coat tail and followed him into the cave. The cave stretched away through the mountain and out the other side.

Micah and Georgio emerged from the cave into tree dotted fields that rolled away toward the horizon and resumed their journey. By mid-afternoon, the travellers came to a deep ravine. A frail looking rope and plank-built bridge was suspended across it. Georgio looked at the bridge with considerable misgiving. As they rested, Micah wondered how they would cross over the ravine. A dove landed on his shoulder and whispered to him, "You will cross safely by an act of love. But the dove flew off before Micah could ask what act.

Micah got up and walked to the bridge. Georgio feigned a limp and said, "my dear friend, I have sprained my ankle and I am too unsteady and fearful to cross. Take me up and help me for I do love you."

Micah heard Georgio's words but not the hollow timbre of his voice and his heart leapt with joy.

Micah put down his burden and took Georgio on his shoulders. Georgio was a bigger and heavier man than Micah and the going was slow and exhausting, Georgio kept his eyes closed and clung to Micah as the frail bridge swayed from side to side.

As they reached the far side of the ravine, Georgio opened his eyes and they both beheld a river that seemed to come from nowhere and stretched away to eternity. The river glinted in the sunlight like gold.

"This is it, I know", Micah sighed, "and how like the bridge is to that thin strand that holds us to life."

"Truly you speak", cried Georgio, "but I will be the first to taste that water!"

And he struck Micah down.

Micah was too exhausted to walk further and lay on the ground, his head reeling from Georgio's blow.

My friend, Micah called after the speeding figure, please help me to the river so that I can be restored.

But Georgio shouted back over his shoulder, "You, I care nothing for you!"

Georgio washed the dirt from himself and scooped the water from the river and drank. A shadow passed across his face and with new-found wisdom he cried out, "I am empty!" As he fell to the ground, he crumbled to dust.

Micah thought his heart would break.

An eagle dived into the river and wet its wings. It sprinkled Micah with the water and gave him water to drink. Micah was restored to health.

"What need you of a false friend", the eagle said, "when you have the constant love of God?"

3-
A Romany Dictionary

The Romany Language (also called Gipsy) is related to the North Indo-Aryan, or Indic, languages. The main concentration of Romany speakers is in Eastern Europe although it is spoken on all five continents. It is not spoken so much in England anymore and there are many true born Romanies who can't speak more than a few words of it. The Romany Language, like its speakers, has seldom received any legal recognition.

The evidence from comparative linguistics is that Romany separated from related North Indian languages in about AD1000. There are thirteen modern Gipsy dialects classified according to their European originals. The language has also accepted many loanwords from native languages.

The vowel and consonant systems of all Romany dialects are derived from Sanskrit and some of the changes in these correspond to those undergone by modern Indian languages. Others represent a more archaic form.

The Romany grammatical system is analogous to that of the modern North Indian languages. The language has five tenses; present, imperfect, perfect, pluperfect and future. It also has three persons.

One aspect of the Romany Language that is quite unique and underlines their attitude to the world and to time is that many Romany words mean opposites. Kaliko means both tomorrow and yesterday, kennadoi means now and then, loko

93

means heavy or light, and meriben means life and death (in a sense, the condition of being one thing or the other.) Some Romany words have found their way into commonly used English slang such as mush (man), kushti (or kushto - good) and balor (literally pigs - policemen.)

The Romany vocabulary reflects the wanderings of its speakers. There is no tradition of writing in Romany, it is a rich oral tradition. Probably the main reason for its survival is that it is useful as a secret language.

A

acai = here
acoi = here
acovo = this
adduvel = that
adenna = then
adoi = there
adovo = that
adre = in
adree = in
adrin = in, inside
adrom = away
adul, adullo = that
adusta = enough
afta = seven
agal = before, in front of
ajaw = good enough
a-jillo = gone
akai = here
akonya = alone
alay = down
amandi = we, us
amen = among
amendi dui = we two
an = on
anava = I bring
anerjal = over against
Anglaterra = England
ankair = to begin
anner = to bring
annerela = it brings
anpali = back again
anvias = came on
ap - up, upon
apopli = back again

arati = by night
asa = so also
asarla = so, thus, also, as
asti = would have, had to
astis = can, possible
asti si = it can be
atch = to remain, stay
atrash = afraid
atukno = sorry
atut = across
av = come
avakai = come here
avali = yes
avava = will come, I come
avella (vela) = he, she, or it
  is coming
avellan = they are coming
avenna = they come
aver = a comer, one who
comes
avessa = thou comest
avo = yes
avri = away, out of
awali = yes
awer = but

B

ba = brother, friend
bai = sleeve, bough
babalo-dye = grandmother
babus = grandfather
bak = luck
bakelo = hungry
bakengro = shepherd

bakro = lamb, sheep
baktalo = lucky
bal = a hair
ballor = hair
balno = hairy
ballovas = bacon
balo = a pig
balor = pigs (also slang for a policeman)
baulo = a hog
bar = hedge, a garden, a pound, a stone
bari = a snail
baro = great
barvelo (m.) barveli (fem.) = rich
baw = brother
bavel = air, wind, breath
bavol = dust
baz = back, behind, open
beeno = born
beng = the devil, flame
bengalo = devilish
bengis = the devil
bengis his zi = the devil in his heart
berk = breast
bero = ship, boat
besh = to sit, a year
beshava = I sit
beshela = he sits
beshdas = he sat
beshdum = I sat
beshed alay = he, she, or it sat down
beshella = he sits, to sit

beshellan = they sit
beshermengro = judge, magistrate, one who sits
beshin = sitting
beshor = years
beshtolay = to sit down
bibi = aunt
bikin = to sell
bikinava = I do or will sell
bisa = poison made from beans
bisser = to forget
bitcher = to send, to emit
bitcherin-kers = police or assize courts
bitcherin-mushor = magistrates
bitcher padel = to transport
bitti = a bit, a little, small (fem.)
bittider = fainter, lower (voice), less, smaller
bitti-mullya = goblins
bitto = a bit, a little, small
bivan = raw, uncooked
blan = wind
bockalo = hungry
bonger = to duck, bend, bow, dodge
bongo = bent, bowed, crooked, unwilling
booti = very
bor = a hedge
boried = it weighed
boro = great (borro)
borodir = greater

boro'in = growing
boro-panni tem = the south
   (literally, ocean-land)
Bori kitchema = Grand
   Hotel
bori pani = the ocean, the
   great water
bosh = a fiddle, to bark,
   noise
boshomengro = a fiddler, a
   fiddle
boshto = a saddle
bothie = a tent
brishin = rain
bruno = brown
bud = after
buddika = a shop
budeskro = a successor
bukko = liver
buller = to boil
bullerin = boiling
bunner = to shape, build
bunnerin = building
buno = proud
but = very, much, often
buti = very, many
butider = more
butidusta = plenty
butiengro = a workman
butsi = work

C

'cai = here
cams = he loves

caulo = unwilling
cavacai = this, here
chai (chi) = girl
chairus = time
chal = a Gipsy lad
chalava = I touch
chalor = Gipsy lads
cham = cheek. leather, tin
chamor = cherries
chamyor = cheeks
char = to pour out, vomit
char = grass
charava = I touch, vex,
   cover, wrap
charo = a dish, plate
chavali = boys, mates
chavey = girl child
chavo = boy child
chavi = child (fem.)
chavor = children
chavorli = here, children!
   mates
chavori = chicken
cheirus = time
cheirusses = times
cherus = time
chi = girl (pron. chy)
chib = tongue, boastful
chichi = nothing
chikk = ashes, dirt, sand
chidom = I put, placed,
   stuck, laid
chin = to cut, to write
chinamangri = a letter
chingari = a row, a quarrel
chinger = through

chinger = to tear, to scold, to quarrel, tear
chingaror = sparks
chinnin peggor = cutting skewers
chiriclo = a bird (masc.) The Romany chiriclo or Gipsy bird is the Water-Wagtail
chiriclor = birds
chirus = heaven
chitti = nothing, trifling, little
chiv = to put, place, fix, throw
chiv apre = to put up, throw up
chiv avri = to put out or away
chivava = I do, or will, put
chivella = he, she, or it puts
chivved = put, placed
chokka = boots, shoes
chommany = something
chone = the moon
chong = knee joint, hill
chor = grass
chore = a thief
chori = poor (fem.)
chorin = thieving
choro = poor (masc.)
chorredo = not of pure Gipsy blood, stolen
chovahani = a witch
choveno = poor
chovihani = a wizard
chovveny = poor

chufa = petticoat, skirt
chukker = to hit together
chukkered = shod, booted
chukko = coat
chuma = to kiss
chumbo = a hill
chumbor = hills
chumer = to kiss
chumor = kisses
chummeny = something
chunger = to spit
churelo = bearded
chureno = poor
churi = a knife
churya = knives
churider = poorer
churdo, churredo = a quadroon, not of pure Gipsy blood, also a poor person, stolen
chury = to climb
churried = climbed
churro = a ball, any round object
chuvveno = poor
chuvveny = poor
coonjerness = secret
coor = to fight, beat, strike
cooraben = a blow, a fight
coppas = things, clothes, blankets, tiles
'covo = this
covva = a thing
covvaben = an incident
crafni = a button, a turnip, a nail

curro = a cup, a tankard
cutter = a bit, drop, rag
cutterengeris = bits, pieces
cuttor = bit

D

dad, dadas, dado = a father
dadeskro = fatherly
dai = a mother
das = gave
de = the
deari = dear
deas = given, gave
deep = pure, accurate,
  correct
deep-dirus = deeper, purer
deepodiridest = deepest,
  purest
del = to give
delaben = a gift
del-apre = to give up, to read
dell = to kick
delled = done, drawn
dellin = hitting or kicking
dellin lescro = "giving it to
  him!"
dell-opre = to give up, to
  read
denne = then
des = gave
desh = ten
dick = to see
dickamengro = a looking-
  glass, mirror

dickavit = to see (tu sasti
dickavit - you should have
  seen)
dickdo = seen
dickdum = I saw
dick kalo = to look glum
dicklo = a handkerchief
dicktum = I saw
dick pali = remember, look
  back
dikk = to wait, to see
dil = a wish
dili = cordially
dilleri = bold, clever
dinnelo = a fool, stupid
diplus = a dimple
dipplor = dimples
divio = mad, insane
divius = mad, insane
divvus = a day (o boro
  divvusko divvus - the Day
  of Judgement)
doeyav = stream, river
'dois = there is
dood = light, a month
dordi = see there, oh dear!
dori = rope, twine, string,
  cord
dovalay = down there
dov'e lo = what is that?
dovo = that
drab = poison, a drug
drabbed = poisoned
drabber = to poison
drabengro = a doctor,
  druggist

dre = in
dre his drom = in his own
way
drom = way, road
dromus = way, road
dromya = roads
droppi = a drop
drumos = a roadway
dud = light, a shooting-star,
moonlight (taley the dud -
by moonlight, divsko dud -
daylight)
dud-bar = diamond
dudikabin = make a clean
sweep, fraud
dui = two
dui-dash (dui-tas) = a cup
and saucer
duiyav = s tream, river
dukk = pain, spirit
dukker = to tell fortunes
dukker = to pain, grieve,
chide
dukkerben = grief, trouble
dukkerin = telling fortunes
dukkerin = tempting
dukkeripen = fortune-
telling, an omen
dukkero = sorrowful
dull = declivity
dum = back
dumbo = a hill
dumo = back
dur = far, long, deep
durmi = among
durodirus = longer, farther

dush = harm, hard
treatment
dush = sorrow
dusher = to harm, injure,
grieve
dusherari = difficult (ma
dusher - don't harm, don't
grieve)
dusheri = hard
Duvel-nasherdo = God-
forsaken
duvels-panni = rainbow
dya = oh, mother!
dye = a mother
dyeskri dye = grandmother

E

engri = added to a word to
qualify a thing
engro = applied to an active
agent
enneah = nine
es = it
esti = for

F

fashni = false, counterfeit
fem = hand
fergoi = fig
ferri = to entice, allure, to
please
ferridiro = better

filissin = a mansion
firstus = first
flick = clever, quick, adept
flicknor = cleverer, quicker
forde = forgive (Miduvel
forde lis - God forgive
him!)
fordia = to be forgiven
fordia wafropen = may his
sin be forgiven
foki = people, folk
fon = from, away, out of
fotografengro = a
photographer

G

gad = a shirt
gajitamos = strangers
garadom = I hid
gargers - Gorgios, non-
Gipsies
gav = a town, a village
gavengro = a policeman
gaver = to hide
gavior = villages, towns
gav-mush = a policeman
gavors = villages, towns
gavver = I do or will hide,
policeman
gavvered = hidden
geero = a man, a person
(non-Gipsy)
ghias = he went
ghiom = I went, we went

ghien = they went
ghilo = gone
gil = to sing
gillaben = a song, a singing
gillas = he sang
gillela = he, she, or it sings
giller = to sing
gilli = a song
gillied = he sang
gillior = songs
ginner apre = to count
Ginny pani = Virginia Water
giv = wheat, oats
givescro = a farmer, farming
givili = a song
giv-puvior = oat-lands
glal = before, in front of
goi = pie, pudding, sausage
gorgiki = Englishwoman
(non-Gipsy)
gorgiko = Englishman (non-
Gipsy)
gorgio = non-Gipsy
gorgiones = in English
graior = horses
granya = a barn
grasni = a mare
gruv = a bull
gruvni = a cow
gry = a horse
gudli = noise, sweetly
gudlo = a trick, sweet, a
sweet thing, sugar
gujer = to make a deep noise
gunno = a bag, sack
guri = to make a noise

gurlo = throat
gurni = a cow
gurniaver = a cucumber
gusveri = wise, discreet
guzno = proud

H

ha = to eat
habben = food
hader = to lift
haddered = lifted
hadem = we ate
hadom = I ate
hafta = seven
halaben = a meal
hamil = to attack
hamlin = kneading
hanik = a well
hanser = to ridicule
haro = copper
hatch = to stand, stay, bring
    (hatch a tan - pitch a tent,
    to hatch it - stand it,
    endure it)
hatched apre = stood up
hatchella = he, she, or it
    stands
hatcherdo = stood, stayed
hatchin = standing
hatch opre = to stand up
haurini = cross, angry
hav = come!
hav acai = come here!
hav avri = come away!

haw = to eat
heb = heaven
hefta = seven (masc.)
hefti = seven (fem. pl.)
hekka, hekki, hokki = haste!
herro, herri = leg, wheel
hev = a hole (coal-hev - a
    coal-hole), a dimple,
    heaven
hevengries = shutters
hevyor = valleys
hevyor = windows
hikker = to confess
hockaben = to lie, a fraud
hockeni = false, fraudulent,
    deceptive, deceit, a lie
hocker = to jump
hockerin = springing,
    jumping
hockerpen = a lie, fraud
hono = angry
hopper = to carry away
hoppercore = policeman
hora = a watch, hour
horra = a penny
hotchella = it burns
hotcher = to burn
hotchered = burnt
hotchewitchi = a hedgehog
hotchni = whiskey
hovalos = stockings
hub = lid, cover
hufa = a cap
hukker = to take away
hukkered = cheered
hukki = already

huler = to shelter
hunkeri = dry
hunkeri-rukk = a dry tree
hunnalo = bored, angry, bad, rotten
hunnalo = obstinate
hunnel = to vex
hunter = to arise
hushti apre = get up
huski = what for? why?
huter = to hang up, to mount
hutered apre = got up (on horseback)
hutlo = shallow
hutto = hang up, mounted
hyver = to look into, to pry into

I

I = she, they
indi = firewood
is = if
iv = snow

J

ja = go
jafra (ajafro) = as such
jal = to go, to make to go (jal the graias = run off with the horses)
jala = he goes

jalan = go on! move on!
jallan = they go
jalls = goes
jampa = frog, toad
jan = for (ja an = go on!)
jassed = gone, went
jassin = going
java = I go, I will go
jaw = go
jaw vri = go away!
jelled = went
jess = go
jessed = gone
jessin = going
ji = to like
jian = they went
jib = language, speech (dre savo jib = in what language?)
jido = living, alive
jiller = to sing
jillo = gone
jin = to know
jinaben = knowledge
jinava = I know
jinavit = to know
jindom = I knew
jins = know
jippo = a patch, patched
jiv = to live
jivaben = life, existence
jivvas = thou livest, didst live
jivava = I live
jivvin = living
jonger = to wake

joter (jota) = together
jove = oats
jukals = dogs
jukalo-Rommanis = dog-
Gipsy
juva, juvo = a wife, woman

K

kai = where
'kai = here
kair = a house, to do
kair lis in kar = do it in
company with someone
kairava = I do, or will do
kairavit = to do
kairdum = I did
kair duro = to sink
kaired kin = tired,
sharpened
kairedo = done
kairen = they make, or do
(so kairen men - what are
we to do?)
kairengeri (fem.) = house-
dweller
kairengro (masc.) = house-
dweller
kairengror = house-dwellers
kairin sig = pretending
kaj = silk
kako = an uncle
kal = cheese
kali (fem.) = black

kaliko = tomorrow, yesterday
kalleri = vain
kalo (masc.) = black, dark,
lazy
kalodirus = blacker
kalo drom = a black road,
dark
kalo pani = the ocean, the
dark or black water
kalopen = darkness, black-
ness
kalo-rattescro = the dark of
night
kam = the sun
kam (pro. came) = business,
affair, want, like, to have
kamakunyo = a mouse
kamava = I love, I like
kamela = he or she loves or
likes
kameli = loving, lovely,
darling
kamescri = loving, a
sweetheart
kamescro = lover
kamlidirest = loveliest
kamlo = loving, darling
kammoben = anything
agreeable (tukey
kammoben - for theie
sake)
kamora, kamorus = a room
kams = he loves, likes
kan = the ear (kanawor =
the ears)

kan, kana = when
kangreski dromya = piety,
  church-going
kangri = church
kangri-pov = churchyard
kani = a hen
kanna = now, when
kanner = to stink
kannis = hens, fowls
kanya = a sack
kap = to take, to get
kap-buti mush = a
  prosperous man
kappa = clothes, a blanket
kar = cry out, roar, shout,
  call to
kari = a thorn, neck
karm = a gleam
kass = hay
kassengro = a hay-stack
katsa = scissors, shears
kauliko = tomorrow,
  yesterday
kaum = to love, like
kavakai = this here
kavi = a pot, kettle
kavodoi = that there
ke = to, that, as
kedi = to pick
kedas = you did
ke-divvus = today
kek = no, not, none
kekavi = a pot, kettle
kek covva = nothing
kek-kek kumi = never no
  more

kekkeno = nothing, none
kekker = no
kekkumi = no more
kek nai = not, there is not
kekumi = anymore
kel = to dance
kelled = danced
kellela = it dances
kellin = dancing
kelloben = a dance, a ball
kenaw, kenna = now, ago
kennadoi = now and then
kenna sig = by and by, soon
kepsi, kipsi = a basket
kepsi kosh = willow
ker = a house
keratti = tonight
keravit = to do
kerdo = done, ended
kerela = he, she, or it does
kerelo = I do
kerimus = doing, deed
kerin = doing
kerm = a worm
kerri = at home
kerro = done, finished
kessur = to care, test, try
  (mandy kessava - I care)
keti = to, towards, straight
  to
kettena, ketteni, kettenus =
together
ki = where, wherever
ki and doi = here and there
kil, kill = to play, to dance
kil = butter

kil-curro = buttercup
killer = to bloom
killin = playing
kin = to buy, the edge
kinlo, kinyo = tired
kipsi = basket
kissi = much (sar kissi - how much?)
kister = to ride
kitchema = an inn
klisin = lock up, to twist about, to wind around spirally
klisin = a key, a lock
ko = what
kokeri (fem.) = self
kokero (masc.) = self
kom = to love, like
kommeni = some, somebody, any
kon = who, then, when, therefore, what
kor = eyebrow
koraben = noise
kor'ben = making a noise
koredo = blind
koosi, kusi = few
kosh, koshter = a stick
koshter-stogg = a rick of faggots
kosser, kusser = to clean
kri-kria, kiri = an ant
krili = funny
kuder = to open
kukalus = doll, fairy, dwarf, goblin

kulla (kolla) = things
kumbo = a hill
kumi = quiet
kun = who, when
kuneri = old
kunjerni = secretly
kunji = narrow, close
kunsus = corner, end
kunter = to adulterate
kur = to strike, beat, fight, to grieve, vex
kuraben = a blow, a fight
kuramengro = a fighting man, warrior
kured = beaten
kurhav = a proverb
kuri = a cup, vessel
kuricus = a week
kurri = tin
kurran = an oath
kurredo = beaten
kurried = beaten
kursas, kurshni = dexterous
kusher apre = to flatter
kushko = good
kushkipen = goodness
kushtier = better
kushtiest = best
kushti-rudered = well-dressed
kushto = good
kushto-bak = good luck
kushtodirus = better
kusno = a basket

L

la = she, her
lab, lav = lip, edge, profit
laj - ashamed
lajipen = shame, modesty
laki = her, of or to her
lakis = hers
langs = along
lasa = her, with her
lassed = he, she, or it took
lastus = at last
latcha = to find, keep
latched, latchdo = found
latchedem = we met, we found
latcher = to find
lati = to her, her
lav = a word
lava = I do or will take
lavengro = a linguist, professor, orator
lavus = a word
le = they
lel = to have, hold, take, to own (yuv lelled a drom - he had a way)
leldom = I took
lellas = you did take
lelled = taken, held, owned
lelled opre = taken up, arrested
lelled adusta = had enough
lellin = taking
lello = taken
lel rak = take care!

lels = he takes
lel vin = take care!
len = they
lender = them, of, from, or by them
lendy = them
lengeris = their, of them
lens = their
les = his
lescro = of him
leskri = of him (proceeds a feminine noun)
lessi = it is
lester = him, of or by him
lesti = to him
lestis kokero = himself
levina, levinor = beer
li = it
lian = you took, got \ lias = he or they took
liom = I took
lil = a book
lilai, lilei = lily, summer, maidenhood
lino = taken
lis = it, him
livinengris = hops
livvena = beer
lo = he, it, that
lock = a shadow
lodder = to lodge, abide
loko = heavy or light
lolo-pabo = tomato
longo-duro = farther
lovver, lovva, lovo, lovvy = money

luchipen = sensuality
ludderin = shaking
lullan = they vanish (len
lullan vri - they vanish
   away)
luller = to vanish, disappear
lullo = red
lullo o' the yora = yolk
lullopen = redness,
   ruddiness
lun = salt
lur = to rob
lutfi chavo = adopted son
lutter = to wallow
luva = money

M

ma = don't
mai = I
maila = donkey
ma-rakker = don't speak
mal, malor, malya =
   companions
maluna = lightning or
   thunder
man = I, the heart, the soul
man = must not, don't!
mander = from me
mandy = I, to me, me
mang = to beg, ask (mi
   mangav tute - I beg you)
mangermengro = a beggar
mano = silly
man pen = mustn't say

mansha to = cheer up!
mansy = with me
manush = a man
manushi = a woman
mariklo = cake
maro = bread
maro's 'ker = an oven
martadas = he wailed
martava = I wail
mas = meat
Mas-divvus = Sunday
masker = in the midst of
matcha = a fish
matchka = cat
matchyor = fishes
matto = drunk
mavi = rabbit
mee, mi = a mile
meeyor, mior = miles
men = among, to me, the
   neck
mendui = we two
mengy = me, to me
mer = to die
mered = died
merela = he, she, or it dies
meriben = death, life
mi = I, me, my
midiri = my dear
Miduvel = God
Miduvelus tem = heaven
mili = sweetly
miller = to add up, assemble,
   mix, adulterate
minner = to make a fuss
minno, minna = my, mine

miraben = life, death
miri = my
miris = mine
misali = a table
mishto = sweet, nice, glad
mishto pen = sweet words
mockardo = depraved
mol, mul = wine (kalo mul - port, lullo mol - red wine)
molengris = grapes
molengri-tan = vineyard
mookerimungeri = tea
mor = do not
mored = killed
moriclo = a cake
mornis, morno = our own
moro = I, our, bread
mortchi = leather
'mout = without
mui = face
muiengri, mui-engro = a picture, a likeness
muk, mukk = to let, to leave, to be worth
mukk alay = to let down
mukkav = let go
mukk mengy jal = let me go!
mukker = to fly
mukkeran duro = flying far
mukkered avri = flown away, let out
mukkered avri his dukk = he delivered himself
mull = worth
muller = to die, to kill
mullered = killed, dead

mullerin = dying
mullo = dead, a bubble, shadow, a spirit, ghost
mullo baulor = dead pig
mull chiriclo = raven (Bird of Death)
mumeli = light, candle
mumper = tramp
mun = the forehead
munella = he, she, or it squeezes
munjer = to pinch, a pig that has died naturally
muscro = a policeman
mush = a man, a mouse
mushero = masculine
mushi = arm
mutchimengro = a tanner
mutterimengri = tea
myla = a donkey
mylas = donkeys

N

naflo = ill, sick
naflopen = an illness
naflopen-kair = a hospital
nak = end
nak o ye divvus = the end of the day
nai = a finger-nail, there is not
nango = bare, naked
narkeri = spiteful
nasher = to lose, to hang,

forget, spoil, run
nashered, nasherdo =
   hanged, lost
nass = away!
nasser = to lean on
nasti, n'asti, nastis = it is
   not, unable, cannot
nav = a name
navvo = named
net = not
nevvi = new
nidderi, nudderi = ignorant
nik-but = no good
nili = blue
nisser = to swallow, to
   remove, empty, extin-
   guish, miss, avoid, keep
   away, pour out, to vex
nisser the beng and sar jivin
   = to swallow the devil and
   every living thing
nisseri covva = strange
   thing
nitchi = peevish
nok = the nose
nosko = ones own
nutti = nuts

O

o (masc.) = the
oitoo = eight
okai, okki = there
opre = on, up
ora = or

ovavo = the other, the next

P

pa = for, on, by, near (hatch
pa leste - wait for him)
pabos = apples
paias, paiass = sport, jollity
paiascro = jolly
pakker = to clean, to defend
pal = a brother
pala = oh, brother!
palaa, pali, palass, pale =
   again, behind
paller = to follow, to nourish,
   to rear
paller an = follow after
palor = brethren
pander = to tie, to suspend
pandered = tied, bound,
   close
panderpen = to pound
panengri = a bell
pani = water
panj = five
panni = water (parl the
panni - over the water)
panser = to approve
papiro = paper
para, puri = to exchange
par-akai = before now
paravit = split, shatter
parl = over, across
parraco = thank you

pash = by, near, beside, a half
pash-divvus = afternoon
pasher = nearly
pash-ajal = neighbouring
pasher a pash bar = nearly half a pound
pash-nili = grey
patoi = a sign
patrin = a leaf
patser = credit, trust, believe
patserdo = trusting
patsered = promised
patserus = possible
patteran, patterani = a track, a sign
pauli = behind, after
pauno (masc.) = white
pauni (fem.) = white
pauvero = poor
peerdos = travellers
peggor = skewers
pekker = to roast, to bake
pelled = fallen
pelled avri = fallen off
'pels it alay = drops it
pelt alay = fallen off
pem = a thing
pen = to say, to think, sister (also a termination of nouns as in Kushto - good, Kushtipen - goodness)
penava = I say
pendas = you said, he said
pendiom = I said

pendos = he said penellen = they say
pennas = thou sayest
pennin = saying
pennis = a saying
pensa, pensi = like, as
per = to fall
pesh = to shine
peski = self
peskri = her own
pessur = to pay
philissin = a mansion
pi = to drink (to pi your kammoken = to drink your health)
pinder = to attack
pingoro = an associate
piopen = drink, something to drink
piredor = travellers, walkers
pirella = he walks
pirengri (fem.) = a traveller
pirengro (masc.) = a traveller
piri = a foot
pirraben, pirriben = a walk
pirried = walked
pirro = beginning (tacho pirro - well begun)
pirro = dear, free, a foot
pirros = feet
pirryin = walking
pirryni (fem.) = dear, sweetheart
pirryno (masc.) = dear, sweetheart

plashta = a red cloak, mantle
poggado = broken
poggado zi = broken heart
pogger = to break
poggerella = he, she, it breaks
poller = to feed, nourish
pooro = poor
poov = the earth, ground, a field
pordo = full
porengripen = writing
pori = a feather, pen or tail
porno = bacon
posh-rat = half-breed Gipsy
posserben = burial
pov = earth, ground, a field
praio-tem = heaven
praler = palor
praller sherro = overhead
prasser = to abuse
praster = to run
prasterin o ye gryor = horseness
puders = it blows
pukk = to say, to speak, to tell, to sing
pukar = aloud
pukeni (fem.) = quiet
pukeno (masc.) = quiet
pukkelan = they tell, they say
pukker = to tell
pukkeras = you tell
pukkerin = telling

pur = to change, to turn
puraben = a turn, the action of turning, exchange
pureni = old age
puri (fem.) = old, aged
puripen = old age
puro (masc.) = old
purr = belly
purub, purus = west
pus = straw
pusheno = buried
pusimegrid = spurred, pricked
pusta = a spur
putch, putcher = to ask
putchin = asking
putsey, putsi = a pocket
puv = earth, ground, a field (plural - puva, puvor)
puv-vardo = plough
pyass = sport, fun, jollity

R

rackli = a girl
racklo = a youth
raffer = to descend
rak, lel rak = take care!
rakker = to speak, to talk
rakli = a girl
raklo = a boy
ran = an osier
rankni = pretty
rani = a lady

ranjer, runjer = to take off, undress
ranya = osier twigs
rashai = a clergyman
rashaior, rashers = clergymen
rashimengro = a preacher
rat = blood
ratfelo = bloody
ratteskri (fem.) = nightly, in the night
ratteskro (masc.) - nightly
ratfully = bloody
rati, ratti = night
rani, rawney, rawni = a lady
religionus = religion
rig (rikk) = side
riggur = to take, carry
rikk, rikker = to keep, to carry, retain
rikkered = kept
rikkers = he keeps, he carries
rikkorus = beside, aside, the side of anything
rinkeni (fem.) = pretty
risher = to bribe
risser = to turn, twist, shake, stir. tremble
riv = to wear
rodder = to seek, search
roi, rooy = a spoon
rokker = to speak
rokkerapen, rokkerpen = speech
Rom = a Gipsy, a husband

Romani, Romeli = a wife
Rommaneskas = Gipsy fashion
Rommani chal = a Gipsy lad
Rommani joter = a Gipsy gathering cry
Rommanipen = Gipsydom
Rommanis = Gipsy language
Rommani, Rommano = Gipsy
romni = a wife
rov = to cry, to weep
rovades = he wept
rovel, rovella = he or she weeps
rudaben = dress
rudderin = seeking
rudela = he or she seeks
ruder = to search, feel the person, seek
ruderpen = dress
rukestamengro = a squirrel (lit. having to do with trees)
rukk = a tree, the gallows
rukker, rukkor = trees
rummer = to marry
rummered, rummoed = married
runjer = to distress
ruppeni = ambitious
ruppeno = silver
rush = clean
rusher = to attack
rushni = bright
ruvv = to weep, cry

ruz = day
ruzh o the sala = dawn
ruzha = flower
ruzhior = flowers
ruzlo = strong, bold, harsh, stiff
ruzno = strong, bold
rya = oh, sir!
rye = a gentleman
ryeskro = gentlemanly

S

sa = such, so, like, as
sa buti = as much as
safran = yellow
sako = all this
sakumi = as ever
sala = the morning
salamanka = a table
salivardo, salivaris = bridle
sani (fem.) = soft
san (masc.) = soft, thin, slender
sap = a drop
sar = all, with, as, like, how
sarapre = all over
sarasar = altogether, always
sarbut = how much?
saridui = both
sarishan (also sarshan) = how do you do?
sarja = everywhere, all
sarlo = morning
saro = all

sarrati = all night
sa saf = all right
sastis = can, able
sasti = perhaps, may be, must, should
satcho = true, truly
sav = to smile, laugh
saveri = cruel
savo = which, that (savo mush - that man)
sav pen la = who says
savver = to laugh
savyins = smiles
se = is
see = heart
selno = green
sensus = since
shab = night, dew
shab o the ratti = to go by night
shaian = perhaps
shak = body, bough, cabbage
shakerella = she covers
sham = evening
sham = I am
shan = you are, they are, bad
shar-apre = to boast
shel = a hundred
shell = to cry or scream out
shellaben = a cry
shells = he cries out
shelled = cried out
sherengro, sherrengro, sherrescro = headman, captain

sherro = head
sherro-bar = headstone
shill = cold
shillaben = a cold
shilleri = cool, chilly
shillo = cold
shillopen = cold
shimal = the north
shindo = wet
shir avri = to pour out
shirki = star
shirro = sour
shock = a bough
shom = I am, shomas = I
    was, mi shom - we were
shom shillo = I am cold
shore = to praise
shorin = praising, boasting
sho-sho = rabbit
shoshoi = a hare or a rabbit
shov = six
shtor = four
shuba = a woman's gown
shukar = quietly, gently, dry
shuker = to whither, fade,
    dry up
shuker = to begin
shul = to whistle
shun = listen
shunaben = obedience, a
    noise, hearing, the sound
    of the voice, pardon,
    judgement
shunalo, shinlo = bad, ill-
    tempered
shunela = she hears

shuned = heard
shunelo = I hear
shuns = sounds
shunum = I heard
shuveni = beautiful
shyan = perhaps
si = as, the soul, heart, be, is
siddi = naughty
sidus = alive
sig = quickly, straight, right,
    way, manner, indication,
    sign, disguise, likeness,
    clour, to be, for, to pity
    (kek sig - no right)
sig, sik o' the tem = the law
sigaben = a chance
sigan = straight on
siggadiro = quicker
sig o my zi = anxious
si kamelo = it is likely
sikker = to show, to teach,
    able, sure
sikkerava = I teach, I show
sikkeras = you teach
sikkerella = he teaches
sikkered = taught
sikkerin = teaching
sikkerin mush = a teacher,
schoolmaster
siklo = used to, accustomed
sim = the same, like, to
    resemble, related
simensa = relations, kin
sims = resembles
sindor = cinders
si pash sig = perhaps

siran = faster
siro puv = a reaped field
siv = to sew, a needle
skammin = chair
skunya = a boot
sleevers = good for nothings
slom = to follow, track
slommado = followed, tracked
slommer = to follow, track
so = what, who
sonaki = golden
sonnakai = gold
soov = to sleep
sor, sore = all
sorno = pork
sos = is, was
so si lis = what is it?
soskeys, suski = what is, why, what
sossi = what is it?
sosti = has to, must, ought
sov = to sleep, to lie down
sovadum = I slept
sovahall = to swear, an oath
sove = to sleep, lie down
sovar = sleepy
spinya = a pin
stadi = a hat (stardi)
stani = buck, stag
stanya = stable
star = to imprison
staripen = prison, imprisonment
starmeskero = imprisoned
staror = the stars

starribened = imprisoned
starya = stars
stekka = a stack
stigga = a gate
suder apre = hung up
suji dovo = what is it?
suker = to burn
sukni = hot
sum = to taste, smell
sumeli = sweet-smelling
suneli = handsome
sunered, sunado = left behind
sur = deep
surni = bright red
surrelo = strong, hard
surriko-mush = an actor
sus = was
sutto = a sleep, a dream
suv = a needle
suvali = infirm
suvo = to sleep, lie down, to swim
swishi = ugly

T

ta = to
tacheni (fem.) = true
tachipen, tachopen = truth
tacho = true, real right
tachodiro = truer
tachonus = true
tader = to draw
tale = under

tamlo = dark
tamlopen = darkness
tan = a place, a tent
taner = to drown
tani (plu. fem.) = small, young
tanopen = childhood, youth
tanya = tents, camp
tarderin = hiding
tas = a cup
tasala = this morning
tasser = to strangle, suffocate, drown
tassered = suffocated, strangled, drowned (beng tasser tute - the devil strangle you!)
tatchi = true
tatter = to heat, fry
tatti (fem.) = hot
tatto (masc.) = hot, handy, expert
tatto-kairaben = sharp practice
tattopen = heat, summer
tav = string, strip, rag
tav apre = to lift up
tawni = little, young
te = and
tel = thread
tem = country
tenna = then
te vel = to come, shall or will (used to express future tense)
tickni (fem.) = a baby, a child

tickno = a baby, a little child (to lel a tickno - to be confined)
tikker = to abide in
tikno = a baby
tir = near
tiro = yours
titla = a butterfly
tiv = to knit
tivdas = she knitted
tivved = knitted
tober = road
toob = grief
tool = to hold, to keep, manage
tooled = held
toolin = driving a cart
toov = grief
tove = to wash
tover = an axe
tovin-divvus = Monday, washing day
trad = care (lel trad - take care!)
trash = fear
trashava = I fear
trasheno (masc.) = awful, fearful
trasheni (fem.) = awful, fearful
trasherdo = afraid, frightened
trasherdo mullo = frightened to death
trashipen = terror, a fearful thing

trin = three
trindesh = thirteen
truppesko = bodily
truppo = the body
trusharo = a pannier
trushilo = thirsty
trushni = a basket
trushul = a cross
tufer = to mend
tukey = to or for you
tukno = sad
tuknus = sorrow
tul = to hold, to drive, squeeze, lead (tul your chiv = hold your tongue)
tulak = behind, back
tule, tull, tuller, tullno = under
tulker = bitter
tullo = fat
tuneri = fierce
tute = you
tuv = smoke, grief

U

-us = a noun termination
utar = west
uzar = by chance

V

vaccasto = lamb
vanka = when

vas = he went, she went
vassavo = bad
vast, vasti = a hand
vava (affix) = will
vias = he came
vin (lel vin) = take care
viom = I came, we came
vonggar = money, coal
voriso, variso = nothing, anything
voro = flour, meal
voudress = a bed

W

wadress = bed
wafli = thin, scanty
wafo, waffodi = bad, evil
waffodi jivvin = bad or hard life
waffodipen = evil
wafodi = bad
wafado, wafro = bad, evil
wafro-dickeno = bad-looking, ugly
wafropen = evil
walin = a bottle, a vessel
walin o dukk = a vessel of wrath
wardo = a cart, van
warfedo = low
warter = to watch, wait
wartni mush = watchman
wast = a hand
wasta-pord = a handful

wastermengris = handcuffs
wastor, wastors = hands
waver = another, the other
waver-temmeny = foreign, belonging to another country
wavero, wavescro = differently, otherwise
wavior = others
welgora = a fair
wellan = they come
wellas = you come
welled ta dukh = come to grief
well-gooro, wellgoro = a fair
wellin = coming
wel, to wel = to come (future tense)
wen = winter
wenesto = wintry
wesh = a forest, a wood
weshengreski = forest ranger
weshengreski chorin = poaching
weshengro = a gamekeeper, a forester
weshni = forested, woody, wild
weshni drom = the road to the forest
weshni-jukal = a fox
weshni-kani = a pheasant
wishto = lip
witchaben = hatred
witcher = to hate

wongish = a little, a short time
wongur = money, coal
wongur-divvus = Saturday, payday
worriso = anything
wuder = a door
wus, wusser = to throw
wye = due

Y

yack = an eye
yag, yog = fire
yagengro = an inspector
yageskro = fiery
yageskro chib = flame, a tongue of fire
yagni = fiery
yak = an eye
yakim = certain, observed, marked
yakk = an eye, a wink (to dell the yakk - to wink)
yakkas, yakkor = eyes
yakkerpen = eyesight
ye = the
yeck, yek = one
yeck covva = one thing
yeck eti waver = one to another
yeckli = only
yeckno = one, single
yeckora, yekorus = once

yek pal' a waver = one to
  another
yiv = snow, ice
yn lach = farewell
yoi = she
yol, yul = they
yoras = eggs
yuv = he
yuv yushered avri = he
  cleared off, vanished
yuzher = to clean

Z

zi = heart, mind, soul
zi-hush = sensible, shrewd,
  sense

4-

Romany Phrases and Proverbs

Tacho like my dad. = True like my father.

Kushto like my dad. = Good like my father.

Yeck mush can lel a grai ta penni, but twenty cant kair him pi. = One man can take a horse to water, but twenty can't make him drink.

A chirrico dree the nast is worth dui dree the bor. = A bird in the hand is worth two in the bush.

Never kin a pong dishler nor lel a Romni by momeli drood. = Never buy a handkerchief nor choose a wife by candle-light.

Always jal by the divvus. = Always go by the day.

Chin tute chuckko by tutes kaum. = Cut your coat according to your fancy.

Fino ranyas kair fino trushnees. = Nice reeds make nice baskets.

Too boot of a mush for his kokero. = He thinks too much of himself.

More covvas the well. = More things to come.

I toves my own gad. = I wash my own shirt. (I am celibate.)

Mo rakker for a pennis when tute cant lel it. = Don't ask for a thing when you can't get it.

The wongurs kairs the grasni jal. = Money makes the mare go.

Its allers the boro matcho that pet-a-lay dree the panni. = It is always the largest fish that falls back into the water.

Bengis your see! Beng in tutes bukko! = The devil in your heart. The devil in your body.

Rikker it adree tutes kokero see an kekll jin it. = Keep it a secret in your heart, and nobody will know it.

Del sar mush a sigaben to kair his jivaben. = Give every man a chance to make his living.

Its sim to a choomer, kushti for kek till its pordered atween dui. = Its like a kiss, good for nothing until it is divided between two.

A cloudy sala often purabens to a fino divvus. = A cloudy morning often changes to a fine day.

Iuzhiou panni never jalled avree from a chickli tan. = Clean water nver came out from a dirty place.

Pale the wafri bak jals the kushti bak. = Behind bad luck comes good luck.

Lel the tacho pirro an its pash kaired. = Well done is half done.

When a mush dels tute a grai tute man dick dree lester mui. = Never look a gift horse in the mouth.

Kair the cammo dearer. = Make the best of it.

The koomi foki the tacho. = The more the merrier.

Hatch till the dood wells apre. = Wait till the moon rises.

The puro beng is a fine mush! = The devil is a nice character.

Mansha tu pal! = Cheer up, brother.

Were lullero adoi we don't jin the jib. = We are dumb where we do not understand the language.

A myla that rikkers tute is kushtier to kistur than a grai that chivs you apre. = An ass that carries you is better than a horse that throws you off.

Si miri chumya shan kushti to ha, tu nasti hatch bockalo, deari, aja! = If kisses of mine were good to eat, you shouldn't go hungry long, my sweet!

5 -

A Romany Yule

Just as lilac was the flower of death, mistletoe that leached from the living tree was never given house room. Mother had a particular dread of poinsettias and any greeting card that bore its garrish image went straight into the fire. The family superstition was that the plant was always, and had proved to be, a harbinger of doom. It is a superstition I still respect.

In the light short days that up to Yule, Pip and I busied ourselves with collecting decorations. We gathered pine cones and chestnuts and bunches of holly and swags of ivy. Pine cones were tipped in bright colours, chestnuts were painted gold and silver and strung on coloured yarn. Tin cans were cleaned, punched with holes, wired and silvered for candle-holders, lanterns hung on the stronger branches of the tree.

The money that Pip and I earned from errands, bottle returns and fruit picking each year was put aside for a few special, store bought gifts and for essentials that could not be made, such as postage stamps and envelopes. Summer's wildflowers, Bindweed, Evening Primrose, Yellow and Scarlet Pimpernels, Cornflowers, Michaelmas Daisy, Autumn Crocus and a collection of bright Autumn leaves had been pressed between sheets of greaseproof paper with a flat iron and, later, carefully stuck on coloured card for Yuletide greetings. We painted and drew other greeting cards and made our own wrapping paper. Mother showed us how to float paints on a water filled tray and lay the brown parcel paper we had saved all year on top of the marbled film.

My postbag was always bigger than Pips. I had found the address of a pen pal agency in the lending library and had become an indefatigable letter writer. Letters and greetings arrived from far and wide. There was something safe in these long distance friendships. The exotic stamps I gave to Pip who had become a serious collector in imitation of our maternal grandfather. As we couldn't afford anything more than surface mail, posting had to be done by the end of October to make sure that letters and greetings reached their destinations in time. The replies taught me much about the world and foreign places and fuelled my wanderlust. I became quite knowledge-able in geography.

Pip and I surrounded our collective presents for Mummy and Da with great secrecy. Our gifts were carefully thought out. Embroidery silks and Eau de Cologne for Mummy, a penknife or neckscarf for Da.

Then, in the weeks before the festive season, the parcels began to arrive. Gifts from relatives, mostly Mummy's, and a big package from our maternal grandparents. New jumpers, books and puzzles, animal-shaped hot water bottles cascaded out on Yuletide morn. Every year the well-to-do family of an American penpal sent me a rich fruit cake covered with walnuts and cherries and sealed in a tin illustrated with scenes by Currier and Ives. Those were how I saw America until I went there.

Autumn was an industrious time of year for Mummy. A constant fug hung over the kitchen where pots and pans bubbled with jams and chutneys. Jars of pickles stood in battalions on the polished cotton tablecloth. Bunches of herbs dried from twine attatched to the kitchen beams.

Yuletide was the time of year that we saw most of Da. For a few days he had the loan of a friends caravan and, fully provisioned, Da, Pip and I roughed it in the wilds. Da taught us both to shoot but, his disappointment was apparent when I refused to hunt. Oddly, I had no such qualms when it came to fishing which Pip and I did through a hole punched in the ice. At times, we had to break the ice in the water butt before we could make the morning tea. Da knew all that there was to know about life and survival in the wild and this he imparted to us, our eyes wide with wonder by yog light at his tales. He came of pioneering stock and came back with tales from the north woods of America. Tales like that of the Windigo, a spirit that walked on feet of flame and stole away men's reason. From Da, I first heard Robert Frost's words -

Whose woods these are, I think I know,
His house is in the village though,
He will not see me stopping here
To watch his woods fill up with snow.

Many years later, I heard the grand old man read his poem on a coming of winter night. I dwelt on his words and on my dim remembered fells as I walked down a leafless Michigan lane. People need hidden meanings. One of the listeners asked Frost what the poem meant, what was it really about between its measured lines. "Meant? About?" Frost replied, "Why, it's about stopping by woods on a snowy evening."

Yuletide eve was always seen in with a supper of kedgery. Before we sealed ourselves away by the hearth, Da took the goose, bartered for with the rabbits he caught and the hares Mummy jugged and jars of homemade conserves, to the baker.

In those days, few people had ovens large enough for the preparation of the Yuletide feast and it was common to have the baker do the lot for a few shillings. The bird, with all its trimmings, was ready to collect early in the morning.

Steaming mugs of cocoa beside the dancing blue flames of pine cones on the Yule log followed supper and it was time for a tale. One in particular was always a favourite of mine and Mummy must have wearied of telling it over and over again.

There was once an old king whose eyesight was failing. One day, while out beside a lake, the old king saw an island. It was the most beautiful island that he had ever seen and he decided that he would have his new castle built upon it. But there was no island. It only existed in the old king's mind.

The old king ordered his architect to build him the finest castle in the land on his new found island. No one dared to contradict the old king and the architect took a boat and rowed to the centre of the lake.

Deep in the lake lived a giant and the architect struck a bargain with him. The giant filled his great hand with mud and stones from the bottom of the lake and raised it above the water.

"There", said the giant, "build your castle. I will sleep for ten years but when I wake, I will claim the castle for my own and carry it to the bottom of the lake."

The architect agreed to the giant's proposition for he would be well paid for his work. He raised a fabulous castle of gold and silver and malachite columns and windows of crystal. Its pennanted towers reached for the sky and the old king was well pleased. For many years, the courtiers enjoyed the lavish life their king provided for them but all knew that this was but borrowed time.

Ten years to the day passed and the old king, now blind, was left alone in his castle because all of his courtiers had fled.

Now, in a hut beside the lake there lived a young widow with her soldiers infant son. The widow heard the story of the enchanted castle and was greatly concerned for the deluded

old king. She placed her son in a boat and rowed to the island. She found the old king walking in his garden. The flowers had stems of silver, leaves of gold and petals of precious stones.

The young widow pleaded with the king to flea to safety but the king did not believe her. The old king was childless and he took the widow's baby in his arms and was very taken with the man child. "Here", said the old king, "you shall want for nothing and I will raise up your child as my son and the heir to my kingdom."

Still the widow begged the king to come away with her and still the king refused and still he would not leave hold of the child.

The widow, distracted with fear, ran to the water's edge. Peering down into the bluey depths, she could see the slumbering giant. The giant began stir and the island and its wonderful castle began to tremble.

The widow could only think to do what she did to calm her infant. She began to sing a lullabye. Her's was a voice of silver sweetness and her haunting melody carried through the depths of the water. The giant nodded and dozed and was soon fast asleep again.

When the old king died, the widow's son became king and he and his mother left the island castle forever.

The giant finally awoke and pulled the castle to the bottom of the lake where it still stands. Only fish swim in its marbled halls, its gleaming towers touched by diving merganzers.

Morning brought the gifting and the collecting of the Yuletide feast. I always took a walk to the wood with the dream of one day finding the magic Eildon Tree percolating in my imagination. The barren trees were hung with icy prisms that bent the sun's warmthless light and the ground was hard with white whiskered frost. All the world slept and He, the protector of all wild things, seemed to sleep too. Only my hymn to Him could conjure all to green.

Sunlight dappled water
The mirror of his laughter
The sparkle of his eyes
The glinting of sunrise
The beauty of his mind
The gift of being kind
The green of leafy bough
Clothes his body now
My verdant lord stood
Worshipped in the wood
Forgiving is the earth
That gives him rebirth.

Beyond the wild wood was the wide world and someday, I knew, I would have to go there. But there are places in the heart to which we all return. Christmas never meant anything to me, but the Pagan spirit of Yule filled my soul.

6 -

Gipsy Songs

Home They Brought Her Warrior Dead

Home they brought her warrior dead:
She nor swooned nor uttered cry:
All her maidens watching said -
She must weep or she will die.

Then they praised him, soft and low,
Called him worthy to be loved,
Truest friend and noblest foe;
Yet she neither spoke nor moved.

Stole a maiden from her place,
Lightly to the warrior step't,
Took the face-cloth from his face;
Yet she neither moved nor wept.

Rose a nurse of ninety years,
Set his child upon her knee -
Like summer tempests came her tears:
Sweet, my child, I live for thee.

Alfred Lord Tennyson

Gipsy Serenade

Merry maid, merry maid, wilt thou wander with me?
We will roam through the forest, the meadow, and lea;
We will haunt the sunny bowers, and when day begins to flee,
Our couch shall be the ferny brake, our canopy the tree.
   Merry maid, merry maid, come and wander with me!
   No life like the gipsy's, so joyous and free!

Merry maid, merry maid, though a roving life be ours,
We will laugh away the laughing and quickly fleeting hours;
Our hearts are free, as is the free and open sky above,
And we know what tamer souls know not, how lovers ought to
   love.
   Merry maid, merry maid, come and wander with me!
   No life like the gipsy's, so joyous and free!

William Harrison Ainsworth

The House-Dweller

You passed me by this werry way,
An' Sarishan? you said to me.
I've often wondered, since that day,
What sort of person you might be?

Says I, "Them's Gipsy words he spoke,
But where could he ha' learnt, and how? -
I don't see much o' Romany folk,
I'm livin in a house, sir, now.

I hate this sort o' life, I do!
I'm Rommany, and want to roam. -
Just fancy! sarishan? from you,
And only English talk at home!

E. H. Palmer

Ten Little Gipsies' Fate

Ten little Gipsies all in a row;
What happened to them I shall let you know.

One little Gipsy climbed up a tree,
Fell down, broke his neck - there lay he!

The second little Gipsy stood upon his head,
And very soon after he was found dead.

The third little Gipsy drank up his ale,
And very soon after was drowned in a pale.

One little - two little - three little Gipsies -
Three little Gipsies they are gone.

The fourth little Gipsy danced himself lame,
Fell down a coal-pit, and up never came.

The fifth little Gipsy was looking at the rain,
And died soon after of thought upon the brain.

The sixth tumbled over a log into the mire,
And afterwards was burnt up to cinders in the fire.

Four little - five little - six little Gipsies -
Six little Gipsies we must mourn.

The seventh little Gipsy ran from a dog,
And very soon after was lost in a fog.

The eighth little Gipsy was always at war
And she was hanged one day in the strings of her guitar.

The ninth little Gipsy was playing with a match,
And very soon after was killed by a witch.

The tenth little Gipsy, who was very, very tall,
Playing Punch and Judy was choked with his call.

Seven little - eight little - nine little Gipsies -
Nine little gipsies all are dead.

Then the doctor whipped his wife,
And shook the little Gipsies till they all came to life.

Ten, nine, eight, seven Gipsies all glad;
Six, five Gipsies dancing like mad.

Four, three Gipsies standing on their heads;
Two, one Gipsies growing like weeds.

Ten little Gipsies all in a row;
What became of them, now you know.

A Gipsy Woman's Song

Look at the Gorgios,
The Gorgios around me,
Trying to take my life,
My life away.

I will wade up to my knees,
Up to my knees in blood,
All for my happy boy.

My husband's taen to prison,
To prison, to prison;
My husbands taen to prison,
To the place of which I know.

The Real Gipsy

Oh! I'm a jolly Gipsy, and I roam the country round;
I'm a real Petulengro as can anywhere be found:
My uncle is a Chilcott, my mother is a Lee,
But I'm the best of all of em, a real Rommany.
    A real Rommany
    From head to foot I be.
Who-op! look into my peepers if a Gipsy you would see!

I go to fairs and races, there I'm always to be found;
One day across the country, then back upon the ground:
One day I'm dressed up swelly, like the gentleman of course,
Then the next I come the beggar, a holding of yer horse.
    "Just a threepence, sir. All right!"
    For I held him jolly tight.
Who-op! I'm the boy as knows the way to run a horse - by
  night!

When a cuttin' of my skewers, so peaceable I am,
You'd say, That Petulengro is the pattern of a lamb!
But I'm handy with my maulies, as I many a time have
  showed,
An can do for any traveller as goes upon the road.
    Oh! at fightin I'm at home,
    Quick to dodge an quick to come;
For at hittin' or at shyin' I'm an out-an-outer Rom!

"How are you, my sweet lady? How are you my lord?" I say:
My wife'll take your money when she comes along this way.
You'll want to give her something - just to keep away the cold-
So I'll step round the corner while your fortunes bein' told.
    Then there'll be a patterin',
    An' an awful chatterin!
So I bid you all good evenin' 'till I come this way again.

Charles G. Leland

A Gipsy Song

"Oh, where have you been, my bonny lad?"
"Oh, I have been up at the fair, my boys,
    With a hack to sell,
    And I cheated a swell,
And all for the love of the Gipsy Boys!"

"Oh, where have you been, my pretty maid?"
"Oh, I have been up at the town, my boys;
    And a fortune I've told,
    And this chicken behold,
Which I stole for the love of the Gipsy boys!

Oh, where have you been, old mother, today?
Oh, I have been up at the farm, my boys;
    And I needn't say how
    I poisoned a sow,
And all for the love of the Gipsy boys!"

"Oh, where are you now, my fiddler lad?"
"Oh, I am all here at hand, my boys;
    And I'll scrape the strings,
    While the romali sings,
And all for the love of the Gipsy boys!"

E. H. Palmer

Fortune -Telling

Cross the poor old Gipsy's hand now
With a little bit of gold;
You've the best of luck, my lady,
That the stars have ever told.

There's a fair young man as loves you,
And you love him fond and true;
There's a dark young fellow also,
Dyin' all for love of you.

And you'll marry him you love, miss,
And you'll make a first rate wife;
You'll be mother of two children,
And be happy all your life.

And if I can read the stars right,
You will meet him here today -
Look! here's someone just a comin
As will bear out all I say.

Shall I tell your fortune too, sir?
What? I can't! - Oh, yes I can.
Don't you laugh at fortune-telling:
Twas with that the world began!

E. H. Palmer

138

Dead Pig

I went to the farmhouse
Where I knew a pig had died,
And to get it I emplored 'em
Till I pretty nearly cried.

But the lady wouldn't give it,
And she 'inted rather free
As twas poisoned by some Gipsy,
And that Gipsy man was me.

Charles G. Leland

Gipsy Morals

A Gipsy lad in his tent did lie:
"How do ye do, my boy?" Said I.
He laughs outright, and says, says he,
"Things is a-goin all right with me,
I'm drunk as a gentleman need to be!"

The girl she gave the fire a poke;
Into the tent came clouds of smoke;
"Bother it! I can hardly see,
The smoke has got into my eyes", says he,
As drunk as a gentleman need to be.

Out of the tent he bundles quick,
And takes the fiddle and fiddle stick;
Down on the grass outside sits he,
Singing away in Rommany -
As drunk as a gentleman need to be.

The Gorgios, when they heard the sound,
Came running up, and crowded round
To hear him sing in Rommany,
Crying, "Oh, look at Mister Lee,
Drunk as a gentleman need to be!"

The Gipsy's daughter was standing by,
And, hearing him sing, began to cry;
"Oh! stop his singin", she says, says she,
"A-teachin of Gorgios Rommany -
As drunk as ever a man can be"

I went and whispered in his ear,
Took him inside to have some beer;
Says I, "I've got a shillin, see!
Send for a gallon, and you and me
Will drink till we're drunk as gents should be."

I saw a clergyman t'other week,
A black-coat fellow with lots of cheek;
"You oughtn't to drink no beer", said he;
Says I, "You're a-tellin a lie to me,
You're as drunk yourself as a man can be."

I loves to see a Gipsy lad
A-singin and playin away like mad;
But this is what seems a sin to me,
To talk afore Gorgios in Rommany,
If a man is as drunk as a man can be.

E. H. Palmer

A Gipsy Song

What care I for my house and land?
What care I for my treasure, O?
What care I for my new-wedded lord,
I'm off with the raggle-taggle Gipsies, O!

Last night you slept on a goose-feather bed,
with the sheet turned down so bravely, O!
And tonight you'll sleep in a cold, open field,
along with the raggle-taggle Gipsies, O!

What care I for a goose-feather bed,
with the sheet turned down so bravely, O!
For tonight I shall sleep in a cold, open field
along with the raggle-taggle Gipsies, O!

Walter Starkie

7 -

Samhain

The copious pages of my journals and notebooks have all gone into the cauldron and been simmered down and the residue is this and *A Romany Tapestry*. I have considered it all with the ghost of my humanity because the caged bird never sings so sweetly as the one in the tree. The years between and the years behind have been quite another story. In the seemingly eternal turgid sea of culture change, the Romany clings tenaciously to the raft of a deeply rooted heritage. It is a very unique heritage.

The personal strands that have tied my survey together have a remoteness now. They are just whispering images unlocked from time and distance. But before memory closes the door for good and all, I take one last flight on the wings of my boyhood imagination. Perhaps it wasn't a dream that I recall. Perhaps it only appears to be when seen through time's diaphanous veil. Whether a dream or not, this particular memory is the testament of my faith.

I have in mind a late Autumn late afternoon with the tingle of coming winter on the tip of the nose. I have missed the school bus home, held back by a vicious, repressed nun intent on punishing me for being, in her words, a heathen. Poor thing, I can feel now, dried up in the unquestioning service of a god who did not bestow on her the gift of eternal youth that mine bestowed on me.

At first there was the pang caused by the sight of my brother Pip's concerned face pressed against the rear window of the retreating bus. Of that time, he was my only and closest friend and the lanolin scent of his woollen jumper lingers in the nostrils of my subconsciousness.

Then, there was the shuddering realisation that it would be dark long before my long walk home ended. Then, the hunger for my delayed tea - a special Sahmain tea when an extra place was set at table for Death. "So that he doesn't take one of our seats", my father would say. No, unless Da could find me, for me there were just grinning jackos on fence posts, corn dollies nailed to barn doors, the distant glimmer of bonfires and the creeping cold of an October night.

I had a choice. There were two roads. The main road, such as it was, was longer. The other road was no road at all. It was a path that led across country through the wood but it was the shorter distance. And so I made then the choice I've made all of my life. I took the road less travelled by.

Dusk clung to the fields until I reached the wood and then the dark began to close in. Pip and I knew that woodland path well enough by daylight but it strangely unfamiliar in the dark. The dark was made darker by an overcast sky and the cold was made colder by a descending frost.

Sometimes I walked at a steady pace but sometimes panic seized me and I broke into a whining run. Skeletal branches snagged my red woollen jumper. Thorns tore my trouser legs and unblinking eyes watched me from the trees as strange sounds ripped away any sense I had of the real.

Eventually, tiredness coupled with a numbness crept up on me unawares. Soon, only the thought of sleep occupied my mind. The tears that confused fear with frustration in unsteady streaks had begun to dry on my face as I slumped down on a mossy patch beneath a wide boled oak.

144

As I drifted, the clouds drifted from the moon and the forest flooded with light, a light more of shadows than of substance. I don't know if I slept, I don't know if I dreamed, I just know, and still with undying certainty know that I saw Him. He stood silhouetted against the moon and his shadow fell across me. He remained motionless in his antlered beauty, his hooves rooted to the ground, and seemed to contemplate me for the longest time. Then, he stooped and pulled me up into his cabled arms and held me tight against the feathery down on his chest. I could feel the moist warmth of his breath coming like wreathes of smoke against my cheek. I knew I had nothing to fear and resigned myself to being carried away.

Da found me lying on a bench in the bus shelter on the main road not more than half a mile away from home. I can still feel the brush of his moustache on my cheek and the oily silkiness of his wavy black hair gripped by my tingling fingers.

Pip plied me with sweetmeats and milky tea as I was rubbed warm and slid into a flannel nightshirt in front of the kitchen range.

I stammered out my tale. I stammered then. And mother was all concern. Da simply said, "Don"t fret, it will pass. He merely saw a deer. The woods are full of them at this time of year. They start to come down from the fells in search of food."

Mother came to me as I lay wakeful. "But I did see Him Mummy and he did help me. I'm sure he said something to me soft and low but just when I think I've got the words, they slip away from me."

"Yes my wild heart", mother drew me to her, "I know you saw Him and I know He helped you. Just as He will always help you if you keep faith with Him." And I have done. I have kept faith with Him and will keep faith with Him until He comes again and I can ask Him, "Wast well done, master?" And as he leads me into the forest, He will say, "Wast well done, my son, and now, at last, you shall be free."

Some other titles published by Capall Bann:

A Romany Tapestry   by Michael Hoadley
"Beautifully and honestly written..light and refreshing.." Old Glory
Always interested in alternative lifestyles and alternative medicine, Michael Hoadley started collecting Romany lore and remedies. This book is the result of a lifetime's association with Romany Gypsies, much of it written from a personal point of view. This is a comfortable, fireside book with something to interest everyone - Romany origins, practices, beliefs customs and lore, healing remedies and tales. An intensely personal book about a little-known people who live life to the full in their own very individual ways.
ISBN 186163 067 0   £7.95

Song of the Earth - Native American Lore and Legend
by Michael Hoadley
Michael Hoadley has had the advantage of being brought into contact with many cultures and many beliefs. Here he relates stories and legends of the native Americans, as taught to him first-hand, illuminated and brought to life with his own insights and personal experiences. A section on herbal remedies is also included together with numerous of his excellent illustrations.
ISBN 186163 1154

Crowning Disasters by Yeoman Warder Geoffrey Abbott
As a member of the Queen's Bodyguard of the Yeoman of the Guard Extraordinary (Beefeater) Geoffrey Abbott is well qualified to write books on strange happenings at regal events. The topics covered in this fascinating book range from the hilarious to the unlikely and in some cases quite macabre. Contents include: SLIP-UPS AT THE CEREMONY things that went wrong at coronations, both English and foreign; OMENS AND AUGURIES when disasters occurred during a monarch's reign, the "I told you so' brigade was quick to identify omens which foretold them; Charles I wore white instead of purple when crowned and so lost his head; George III lost a jewel from his crown, later lost America; FEASTS AND AFFRAYS coronation banquets which frequently ended in chaos, riots and looting; table manners of the day; royal menus; FINERY, FASHIONS AND FRIPPERY coronation robes and their ultimate fate - sold; given to Mme Tussaud's; used in plays; SLEAZE FOR SYCOPHANTS perks for parasites, favours for flatterers, titles for toadies; James I 'hunted everything that ran and knighted everything that crawled' created 400 new knights, a notice later appearing at St Paul's sarcastically offering memory lessons to those who had to announce them; PALACE PASTIMES flirting and wooing, masques and mistresses, dice-playing, jesters, and other right royal entertainments; ROYAL ODDITIES regal pretenders and their fate; the English queen tried for witchcraft; coronation medals; duties of the Yeomen of the Guard; attempted assassinations; Napoleon Bonaparte once a London Special Constable! APPENDICES- Royal letters   ISBN 186163 1324

FREE DETAILED CATALOGUE

Capall Bann is owned and run by people actively involved in many of the areas in which we publish. A detailed illustrated catalogue is available on request, SAE or International Postal Coupon appreciated. **Titles can be ordered direct from Capall Bann, post free in the UK** (cheque or PO with order) or from good bookshops and specialist outlets.

Do contact us for details on the latest releases at: **Capall Bann Publishing, Freshfields, Chieveley, Berks, RG20 8TF.** Titles include:

A Breath Behind Time, Terri Hector
Angels and Goddesses - Celtic Christianity & Paganism, M. Howard
Arthur - The Legend Unveiled, C Johnson & E Lung
Astrology The Inner Eye - A Guide in Everyday Language, E Smith
Auguries and Omens - The Magical Lore of Birds, Yvonne Aburrow
Asyniur - Womens Mysteries in the Northern Tradition, S McGrath
Beginnings - Geomancy, Builder's Rites & Electional Astrology in the
      European Tradition, Nigel Pennick
Between Earth and Sky, Julia Day
Book of the Veil , Peter Paddon
Caer Sidhe - Celtic Astrology and Astronomy, Vol 1, Michael Bayley
Caer Sidhe - Celtic Astrology and Astronomy, Vol 2 M Bayley
Call of the Horned Piper, Nigel Jackson
Cat's Company, Ann Walker
Celtic Faery Shamanism, Catrin James
Celtic Faery Shamanism - The Wisdom of the Otherworld, Catrin James
Celtic Lore & Druidic Ritual, Rhiannon Ryall
Celtic Sacrifice - Pre Christian Ritual & Religion, Marion Pearce
Celtic Saints and the Glastonbury Zodiac, Mary Caine
Circle and the Square, Jack Gale
Compleat Vampyre - The Vampyre Shaman, Nigel Jackson
Creating Form From the Mist - The Wisdom of Women in Celtic Myth and
      Culture, Lynne Sinclair-Wood
Crystal Clear - A Guide to Quartz Crystal, Jennifer Dent
Crystal Doorways, Simon & Sue Lilly
Crossing the Borderlines - Guising, Masking & Ritual Animal Disguise in the
      European Tradition, Nigel Pennick
Dragons of the West, Nigel Pennick
Earth Dance - A Year of Pagan Rituals, Jan Brodie
Earth Harmony - Places of Power, Holiness & Healing, Nigel Pennick
Earth Magic, Margaret McArthur

Eildon Tree (The) Romany Language & Lore, Michael Hoadley
Enchanted Forest - The Magical Lore of Trees, Yvonne Aburrow
Eternal Priestess, Sage Weston
Eternally Yours Faithfully, Roy Radford & Evelyn Gregory
Everything You Always Wanted To Know About Your Body, But So Far
    Nobody's Been Able To Tell You, Chris Thomas & D Baker
Face of the Deep - Healing Body & Soul, Penny Allen
Fairies in the Irish Tradition, Molly Gowen
Familiars - Animal Powers of Britain, Anna Franklin
Fool's First Steps, (The) Chris Thomas
Forest Paths - Tree Divination, Brian Harrison, Ill. S. Rouse
From Past to Future Life, Dr Roger Webber
Gardening For Wildlife Ron Wilson
God Year, The, Nigel Pennick & Helen Field
Goddess on the Cross, Dr George Young
Goddess Year, The, Nigel Pennick & Helen Field
Goddesses, Guardians & Groves, Jack Gale
Handbook For Pagan Healers, Liz Joan
Handbook of Fairies, Ronan Coghlan
Healing Book, The, Chris Thomas and Diane Baker
Healing Homes, Jennifer Dent
Healing Journeys, Paul Williamson
Healing Stones, Sue Philips
Herb Craft - Shamanic & Ritual Use of Herbs, Lavender & Franklin
Hidden Heritage - Exploring Ancient Essex, Terry Johnson
Hub of the Wheel, Skytoucher
In Search of Herne the Hunter, Eric Fitch
Inner Celtia, Alan Richardson & David Annwn
Inner Mysteries of the Goths, Nigel Pennick
Inner Space Workbook - Develop Thru Tarot, C Summers & J Vayne
Intuitive Journey, Ann Walker Isis - African Queen, Akkadia Ford
Journey Home, The, Chris Thomas
Kecks, Keddles & Kesh - Celtic Lang & The Cog Almanac, Bayley
Language of the Psycards, Berenice
Legend of Robin Hood, The, Richard Rutherford-Moore
Lid Off the Cauldron, Patricia Crowther
Light From the Shadows - Modern Traditional Witchcraft, Gwyn
Living Tarot, Ann Walker
Lore of the Sacred Horse, Marion Davies
Lost Lands & Sunken Cities (2nd ed.), Nigel Pennick
Magic of Herbs - A Complete Home Herbal, Rhiannon Ryall
Magical Guardians - Exploring the Spirit and Nature of Trees, Philip Heselton
Magical History of the Horse, Janet Farrar & Virginia Russell
Magical Lore of Animals, Yvonne Aburrow
Magical Lore of Cats, Marion Davies
Magical Lore of Herbs, Marion Davies

150

Magick Without Peers, Ariadne Rainbird & David Rankine
Masks of Misrule - Horned God & His Cult in Europe, Nigel Jackson
Medicine For The Coming Age, Lisa Sand MD
Medium Rare - Reminiscences of a Clairvoyant, Muriel Renard
Menopausal Woman on the Run, Jaki da Costa
Mind Massage - 60 Creative Visualisations, Marlene Maundrill
Mirrors of Magic - Evoking the Spirit of the Dewponds, P Heselton
Moon Mysteries, Jan Brodie
Mysteries of the Runes, Michael Howard
Mystic Life of Animals, Ann Walker
New Celtic Oracle The, Nigel Pennick & Nigel Jackson
Oracle of Geomancy, Nigel Pennick
Pagan Feasts - Seasonal Food for the 8 Festivals, Franklin & Phillips
Patchwork of Magic - Living in a Pagan World, Julia Day
Pathworking - A Practical Book of Guided Meditations, Pete Jennings
Personal Power, Anna Franklin
Pickingill Papers - The Origins of Gardnerian Wicca, Bill Liddell
Pillars of Tubal Cain, Nigel Jackson
Places of Pilgrimage and Healing, Adrian Cooper
Practical Divining, Richard Foord
Practical Meditation, Steve Hounsome
Practical Spirituality, Steve Hounsome
Psychic Self Defence - Real Solutions, Jan Brodie
Real Fairies, David Tame
Reality - How It Works & Why It Mostly Doesn't, Rik Dent
Romany Tapestry, Michael Houghton
Runic Astrology, Nigel Pennick
Sacred Animals, Gordon MacLellan
Sacred Celtic Animals, Marion Davies, Ill. Simon Rouse
Sacred Dorset - On the Path of the Dragon, Peter Knight
Sacred Grove - The Mysteries of the Forest, Yvonne Aburrow
Sacred Geometry, Nigel Pennick
Sacred Nature, Ancient Wisdom & Modern Meanings, A Cooper
Sacred Ring - Pagan Origins of British Folk Festivals, M. Howard
Season of Sorcery - On Becoming a Wisewoman, Poppy Palin
Seasonal Magic - Diary of a Village Witch, Paddy Slade
Secret Places of the Goddess, Philip Heselton
Secret Signs & Sigils, Nigel Pennick
Self Enlightenment, Mayan O'Brien
Spirits of the Air, Jaq D Hawkins
Spirits of the Earth, Jaq D Hawkins
Spirits of the Earth, Jaq D Hawkins
Stony Gaze, Investigating Celtic Heads John Billingsley
Stumbling Through the Undergrowth , Mark Kirwan-Heyhoe
Subterranean Kingdom, The, revised 2nd ed, Nigel Pennick
Symbols of Ancient Gods, Rhiannon Ryall

Talking to the Earth, Gordon MacLellan
Taming the Wolf - Full Moon Meditations, Steve Hounsome
Teachings of the Wisewomen, Rhiannon Ryall
The Other Kingdoms Speak, Helena Hawley
Tree: Essence of Healing, Simon & Sue Lilly
Tree: Essence, Spirit & Teacher, Simon & Sue Lilly
Torch and the Spear, Patrick Regan
Understanding Chaos Magic, Jaq D Hawkins
Warriors at the Edge of Time, Jan Fry
Water Witches, Tony Steele
Way of the Magus, Michael Howard
West Country Wicca, Rhiannon Ryall
Wildwood King , Philip Kane
Wondrous Land - The Faery Faith of Ireland by Dr Kay Mullin
Working With the Merlin, Geoff Hughes
Your Talking Pet, Ann Walker

FREE detailed catalogue and FREE 'Inspiration' magazine

Contact: Capall Bann Publishing, Freshfields, Chieveley, Berks, RG20 8TF